T0294194

KEN PYE

EVEN MORE MERSEYSIDE TALES!

CURIOUS & AMAZING TRUE STORIES

FROM HISTORY

The History Press

First published 2023

The History Press
97 St George's Place, Cheltenham,
Gloucestershire, GL50 3QB
www.thehistorypress.co.uk

British Library Cataloguing in Publication Data.
A catalogue record for this book is available from the British Library.

ISBN 978 1 80399 203 7

Typesetting and origination by The History Press
Printed and bound in Great Britain by TJ Books Limited, Padstow, Cornwall

MIX
Paper from
responsible sources
FSC
www.fsc.org FSC® C013056

Trees for Life

CONTENTS

INTRODUCTION

In my first two volumes of *Merseyside Tales* I stated just how proud I am of being a born-and-bred Scouser, but one who has worked all over Merseyside and who loves the entire county with an abiding passion – even though it is now officially known as Liverpool City Region. One of the many things that make this part of the world so attractive for me, apart from its wonderful people, is its rich and diverse heritage. While I find this endlessly fascinating, I am particularly entertained and continuously amazed by the wealth of tales from its history that I find odd, unusual, surprising, impressive, or simply bizarre.

This is the third volume in my series of such stories, and here you will find another fifty-five that I am sure will entertain, delight, and hopefully surprise you too. As with my previous volumes, each of the stories is true (although some are more true than others!) and they all prove that, indeed, 'truth is stranger than fiction'. I certainly hope that you enjoy reading them, just as much as I enjoyed researching and writing this, my collection of *Even More Merseyside Tales!*

Ken Pye FLHU
Liverpool, 2023

The author and his family. (Discover Liverpool library)

1

ᾘHE ᾙUGNACIOUS VICAR OF ᾘUYTON

'Muscular Christianity' was a term used to describe powerful, blood-and-thunder, hellfire-and-damnation preaching in Christian churches, especially during the Victorian era – although quite a bit of this still goes on today! In the nineteenth century, one of the best exponents of this style of sermon was one of the vicars of St Michael's Church, on Bluebell Lane in Huyton village. This has always been an important site of worship, probably even in Pagan times, and there has been a church on this site from at least the twelfth century. The present building dates from 1663 and is Grade II listed.

Many redoubtable vicars have ministered at St Michael's over the years, and the longest serving to date was the Reverend Ellis Ashton (1789–1869). He was vicar for fifty-six years, between 1813 and 1869, and a local road is named after him. He was a member of the very wealthy Ashton family and was born in the grand family home of Woolton Hall, in Liverpool.

Reverend Ashton had a reputation for being a forthright and dominating personality, and he was appalled that the young men of his parish were using the village green, in front of his church, for cockfights and for the even more bloodthirsty 'entertainment' of bull baiting. So angered was he by this that he delivered many sermons condemning the practices and the gambling that went with them.

However, his preaching fell on deaf ears, so one day when there was a major bull-baiting bout taking place on the land in front of his church, he took off his coat, rolled up his sleeves, and marched out of his church and directly onto the green. He then proceeded to belabour each of the offenders, quite impressively getting the better of even the

Bull baiting. (Liverpool Athenaeum library)

biggest youths, who were all too ashamed and intimidated to take on their vicar, who was a big man!

The blood sports now stopped for good and church attendance increased, especially among the young men of the village. The forceful vicar had given a whole new meaning to the phrase 'muscular Christianity'!

Although St Michael's has altered much over the centuries, there are many signs of its ancient history in and around the building. These include two fonts, one dating from the eighth or ninth century and the other from the 1600s. The older font was discovered during repair work in 1872, when it was excavated from beneath the church tower. This was along with a capital from a Saxon stone column, which is decorated with four helmeted heads.

Huyton had become quite an important local market town by the mid-nineteenth century, with a large resident population. As a result, the church graveyard, which had only a limited area, soon filled up. This meant that a branch burial ground was now needed. This was created at the end of Derby Terrace, in the corner of the village green.

One of the reasons why the graveyard needed to expand was that the church also served a number of other local villages and communities.

A remnant of this function can be found a little way down the hill from the church. Here, running opposite the road named The Garth, there is a wide passage. It is all that remains of a long track that once connected the nearby village of Tarbock with Huyton. Records dating from 1520 show that it was along this old pathway that the medieval inhabitants of Tarbock would carry the bodies of their loved ones for burial at St Michael's Church in Huyton village; hence the name of the passage – Corpse Way!

2

THE EARL AND THE PUSSYCAT

Edward Smith-Stanley, the 13th Earl of Derby, was born in 1775, and owned one of the finest, private natural history collections in the world. He also had a large menagerie and aviary. These were all located on his exceptionally large estate at Knowsley Park, which stands near the township of Prescot, just to the east of Liverpool. Here, his current descendant, the 19th Earl of Derby, owns Knowsley Safari Park, so the modern keeping of animals at Knowsley is nothing new!

However, whilst today's safari park is a popular tourist attraction, the 13th Earl's menagerie was only for his personal amusement and the edification of his family and invited guests. In fact, it was he who built the 13-mile-long wall that still surrounds part of the Knowsley Park Estate. This was designed to combat the problem of local people breaking into his collection to poach an emu or a pelican to roast for their Sunday lunch – just for a change!

The 13th Earl was President of the Zoological Society, and in his private zoo he had ninety-four different species of animals and 318 kinds of birds. In 1831, Earl Edward was visiting Regent's Park Zoo in London when he noticed a young man sketching the animals. Lord Derby was so impressed by the young man's artistry and technical accuracy, that he commissioned him to move up to Knowsley to sketch all of the animals. The youth readily agreed, little knowing that the job would take him five years.

Suffering from shyness and social inexperience when he came to Knowsley Park and Hall (he was only 20 years old after all), the youth was out of his depth. However, he became very friendly with the young children of the earl and his relatives and Lord Derby encouraged this. When not engaged on his commission, the artist could often be found in the nursery, playing with and entertaining the youngsters. He regularly kept them amused by drawing humorous sketches and cartoons for them and writing limericks and nonsense verses.

'Can you write a rhyme about anything Sir?' they asked him one day.

'Why, yes, my children,' he replied. 'Simply pick a subject or an object and test me out!'

The children looked around the room and saw, staring balefully at them from the top of a sideboard, one of the earl's great owls. The aristocrat's habit was to stuff and mount the animals in his collection after they had died and display them throughout Knowsley Hall. He even employed a resident taxidermist!

The children pointed and cried out excitedly, 'That Sir; the owl! Can you write about that?'

The young man thought for a few moments, smiled wryly to himself, and then immediately recited, writing and sketching as he spoke:

The Owl and the Pussy-cat went to sea in a beautiful pea green boat.

They took some honey, and plenty of money, wrapped up in a five pound note.

The Owl looked up to the stars above, and sang to a small guitar,

'The Owl and the Pussycat' by Edward Lear. (Discover Liverpool library)

'Oh lovely Pussy! Oh Pussy my love, what a beautiful Pussy you are, You are! You are!

'What a beautiful Pussy you are!'

The name of the young man, of course, was Edward Lear (1812–88), and he went on to publish his limericks and nonsense rhymes to great public acclaim. He also published his sketches of Lord Derby's animals, in 1846, in a volume entitled *Gleanings from the Menagerie and Aviary at Knowsley Hall*. These drawings and watercolours are still acclaimed for their outstanding accuracy, lifelike colour and high quality.

The 13th Earl died in 1851, and once Queen Victoria and the Zoological Society of London had taken 'first pick', he bequeathed his private museum to the people of Liverpool. He also gave part of his vast collection of stuffed animals and birds, including the owl! This collection became the basis of the first Liverpool Museum, which still stands on William Brown Steet in the city. The owl from the 'Owl and the Pussycat' rhyme was, for a time, on display in the Museum of Liverpool at Mann Island, near the Pier Head. However, it has now disappeared, and none of the museum staff could tell me where it has gone!

3

'THE CAZZIE': THE CAST-IRON SHORE

Until the coming of the Industrial Revolution, in the latter decades of the eighteenth century, the full length of the Liverpool waterfront on the River Mersey was largely unspoilt sand and shingle beach. But, with the building of 7½ miles of dense docklands throughout the eighteenth, nineteenth, and twentieth centuries, this was all industrialised and lost forever. Only a small stretch of natural beach remains in the isolated hamlets of Oglet and Dungeon, near the southern district of Speke. However, this too is now threatened by the planned expansion of nearby Liverpool John Lennon Airport.

One of the riverfront areas that was particularly despoiled was the Dingle District, just north of Speke. Even so, a short length of shoreline was not actually built over until the early 1980s. This remained a playground and swimming area for local people until that time. For decades it had been known as the Cast-Iron Shore, or 'The Cazzie', and it is still fondly remembered by many older Liverpudlians.

The name dates from 1815, and refers to the cast iron produced at the vast Mersey Forge Iron Foundry, which stood near the Dingle waterfront on each side of Sefton Street. It had been established in 1810, and produced cast and forged iron. Steel was also manufactured there, using massive, pivoting furnaces called Bessemer converters. There were also huge smelting and puddling yards, great rolling and stamping mills, and a 15-ton steam-hammer. Its persistent thump, thump, thumping was loud enough to be heard in Wirral. Following many complaints, it was finally silenced as the result of a court case.

At its peak of operation, the Mersey Forge employed 1,500 men. It also made armour plating and armaments including, in 1856, the gigantic

The Cast-Iron Shore. (Discover Liverpool library)

Horsfall gun. It was the largest gun in existence at the time, weighing 21 tons 17 cwt. It was tested on Liverpool's North Shore, watched by very large crowds and with the streets decked out with bunting. Everyone witnessed a 300lb ball being shot for a distance of 5 miles.

The massive cannon was intended to be used in the Crimean War, which had been fought since 1853, by Turkey, France, and Britain against Russia. But, to the disappointment of the forge owners and workers, the war ended three days after the gun was finished.

When the Liverpool to Garston railway was being cut through the south docks in 1864, the forge had to move to three new sites, separated by Grafton and Horsfall Streets but connected by long, wide, and very busy tunnels. They are still there beneath the modern streets!

This was a time before the existence of the Health and Safety Executive and before environmental awareness. The ignorance of the people then meant that the spoil from this heavy industry had been allowed to run off and heavily taint and discolour the land all around, including the shore and the rocks. The beach now took on all the colour shades of metal – from yellow and orange through red and blue to grey and black – hence the name then given to the shore by local people.

After the closure of the Mersey Forge in 1898, this section of the river's edge became a very popular swimming spot for local children and young men, and a picnic destination for families. No one minded the colour or pollution in the water or on the Cast-Iron Shore, why would they?

The forge sites were eventually demolished, cleared and built over. Then, in 1982, the Cazzie too disappeared under the bulldozers as building work began on reclaiming the land for conversion into a new riverside walkway and embankment. This would form part of the International Garden Festival: But that is another story!

4

THE PRESCOT TURNPIKE AND THE MOB

Because of Prescot Town's dreadful reputation for unruly behaviour and drunkenness, in 1759, the people of nearby Liverpool became convinced that they were about to be invaded and attacked by mobs of Prescot villains! In October that year, the Corporation of Liverpool appointed a committee to 'appraise and value the arms ... to defend the town from the insults of the Prescot mob'.

In September the following year, the council ordered that 'Mr. Adams, gunmaker, be paid the sume of fourty-nine pounds for a parcel of musketts and bayonets, & c, sold to this Corporation when the town was in danger of being plundered by a mob of country people and colliers in and about Prescot'.

All of this panic had come about because of the tolls that Liverpool had imposed on the coaching road from Liverpool to Prescot, and the fact that Prescot people did not want to pay them! By the beginning of the 1700s, the most important road in and out of Liverpool and its port was the packhorse route to and from Prescot. This was mainly used to transport coal, which was becoming an increasingly important commodity on the eve of the Industrial Revolution.

The state of the road, though, was very poor. The surface was uneven, strewn with rocks and boulders, and full of potholes. When it rained some of these were so deep that people had been known to fall in and drown – very few people could swim in those days. Also, in bad weather the road could become waterlogged and turn into a mire of mud. It was the responsibility of each parish the road passed through to make the road good and usable. Some parishes did and some did not.

As the route became busier, and as other routes began to make their way out of town, something had to be done to enforce road maintenance and security. So, in 1726, an Act of Parliament created the Liverpool to Prescot Turnpike Road. 'Turnpiked' meant that tollbooths, toll gates, or toll houses were placed at various points along a principal packhorse or coaching route. These were to raise income to pay for the regular upkeep of the roads.

A turnpike was originally a gate-like frame, pivoting at one end on an upright post or 'pike'. This was kept closed and blocked the way until a toll was paid. Local constables were employed to secure the roads and monitor the toll houses.

The road charges were paid in addition to any fares that travellers were already paying for their transportation. They were also paid by people who were simply travelling on horseback. Pedestrians were not charged, providing they were not carrying goods, and there were usually side gates through which they could freely pass.

At this time, tolls on the new Prescot Turnpike were:

for wagons carrying coal, 6*d* each;
for carts carrying coals, 2*d*;
for carts carrying other commodities or goods, 6*d*;

A packhorse bringing coal into Liverpool. (Discover Liverpool library)

for horses carrying coal, ½*d*;
for other horses 1d;
for coaches, 1 shilling;
for cattle ½*d* per head;
and for sheep ¼*d* (one farthing) per head.

The toll keepers were called 'pikemen' and they each wore a uniform. This consisted of a tall black hat, black stockings and knee britches, and short aprons with deep pockets in which to hold the money. The wages paid to these men – and sometimes women – were poor, but at least they and their families could live, rent free, in the purpose-built toll cottages.

In the 7 miles between Liverpool and Prescot there were four toll bars. These were located at Fairfield, Old Swan, Knotty Ash, and Huyton. Anyone who tried to avoid travelling through the turnpikes found that others were also installed on branch roads – if you wanted to move yourself or your goods then there was no escape!

No wonder the people of Prescot were incensed by this obstruction to their freedom of movement, and this new financial burden on their commerce. And to think that early in the seventeenth century letters to Liverpool used to be addressed to 'Liverpool, near Prescot'!

5

ᛚIVERPOOL GENTLEMEN AND MANCHESTER MEN

The inland city of Manchester had developed industrially almost in parallel with Liverpool, but its workforce, and that of its surrounding towns, was principally employed in factories and textile mills. It had, however, received its charter as a city in 1853. The port did not achieve its city charter until 1880. Also, its workforce was largely engaged in dock labour and maritime industries. Nevertheless, in relation to Manchester, it had a very large white-collar workforce too. These were mostly the clerks, accountants, insurance agents, and company administrators who were all involved in the running of a large port.

It was said that Liverpool gentlemen imported cotton while Manchester men made it into cloth. This led to the phrase 'Liverpool Gentlemen and Manchester Men', which was then doing the rounds of the gentlemen's clubs, coffee houses, dinner parties and soirées of the north-west. This more than implied some sort of superiority on the part of Manchester's great commercial rival.

What really upset the 'Manchester Men', though, was the level of the dock, harbour, handling, and shipping fees that Liverpool was charging them to process their imports and exports, which they believed were excessive and monopolistic. Something had to be done to cut out the 'middle-men' of Liverpool and bypass the port in some way. A canal from Manchester directly to the sea seemed to be the only realistic solution.

While this idea had been around as early as 1660 – and indeed, Thomas Steers (1672–1750), who had designed and built Liverpool's (and the world's) first commercial wet dock, had also drawn up plans – nothing had happened. But then, in 1882, Manchester engineer

Digging the Manchester Ship Canal. (Liverpool Athenaeum library)

and manufacturer Daniel Adamson (1820–90) called a meeting of Manchester and Cheshire men who could fund such an enterprise. He also brought together other leaders from local businesses, as well as representatives and politicians from towns and communities who would directly benefit from such a canal. These men then put a bill together that they presented to Parliament later that year.

Liverpool naturally objected to Manchester's proposals at every turn, especially in Parliament. However, the persistence of the new canal's advocates, as well as a general desire to take the smugness of Liverpool down a few notches, meant that, eventually, in 1885, a bill was passed in the House and work could now begin on the Manchester Ship Canal.

Edward Leader Williams (1828–1910) was appointed as chief engineer, and the first spadeful of earth was dug on 11 November 1887, by Lord Egerton of Tatton. He had recently taken over the chairmanship of the Manchester Ship Canal Company from Adams.

Actual construction work began in 1888, with an average workforce of 12,000 navvies, and almost 200 steam trains hauling 6,000 wagons. The first stretch, to Ellesmere Port, was opened to the first ships on 1 January 1891, the second stretch, to the River Weaver, opened the following September. Costing £15 million to build, the canal was officially opened by Queen Victoria in May 1894.

The canal begins at purpose-built Eastham Locks on Wirral, directly across the Mersey from Garston in Liverpool. It then stretches for 36 miles (56km) and is, in effect, one long harbour servicing a vast range of industries, factories, businesses, and communities between Eastham and Manchester. Using their own vessels or renting canal space to other shipping lines, the company could not only accept small boats and barges to transport goods and raw commodities, but oceangoing ships too. The canal is wide and deep, so can accommodate ships up to 600ft long (183m), 65ft 6in (20m) wide and almost 28ft (8.5m) deep.

The company also invested in the building of a vast complex of inland docks at Salford Quays near Manchester. However, ships' cargoes could also be processed and serviced at many points along the canal. Container ships could also use the canal, which means that Manchester could keep pace with Liverpool's expansion into this modern form of cargo handling.

Railway lines were laid directly from the Salford Docks and Manchester, and alongside the canal to the rest of Britain, facilitating the movement of goods throughout the country. Liverpool's monopoly was now well and truly broken. This entire operation was controlled from Eastham.

The Manchester Ship Canal connects with the River Bollin, Glaze Brook, the Mersey, the River Irwell, the Bridgewater Canal, the Shropshire Union Canal, and the Weaver Navigation. Significant crossings of the canal include the Mersey Gateway Bridge, the M6, Warburton Toll Bridge, Hulme Bridge Ferry between Irlam and Flixton, the M60, Barton Swing Aqueduct, Latchford Rail Viaduct (closed in 1984), and Barton Road Swing Bridge.

As ships increased in size through the 1950s, particularly oil tankers, they became difficult for the canal to handle. However, they still needed to discharge their cargos of crude oil, and so, in 1954, a new dock was constructed on the landward side of Eastham Lock. Large ships can now bypass the canal entrance, anchor in Eastham Dock, safely discharge their cargo, and return to sea.

The canal is now privately owned by Peel Holdings, whose plans include redevelopment, expansion, and an increase in shipping from 8,000 containers a year to 100,000 by 2030, as part of their Atlantic Gateway project.

Sadly, the totally unnecessary rivalry between Liverpool and Manchester continues, especially between football supporters. However, the City Region Mayors of Liverpool and Manchester are both Scousers who already work well together. They share a vision for commercial, social, industrial, and environmental partnerships between the north's two greatest cities. Both cities are also blessed because they are made up of Liverpool and Manchester Men and Women, and Manchester and Liverpool Gentlemen and Gentlewomen!

6

A Bridge Too Far

Since 1440, the Molyneux family had been holders of Liverpool Castle and its surrounding land, under licence from King Henry VI (1421–71). By 1632, Richard Molyneux (1594–1636), the 1st Viscount, and his family (who went on to become the Earls of Sefton) had leased the rights to the Manor of Liverpool from King Charles I (1600–49).

But this was the time when Puritans and Parliamentary forces ruled England under Oliver Cromwell (1599–1658) and – as a supporter of the Royalists in the Civil War, and having betrayed the town, leading to a massacre of hundreds of its inhabitants – Richard's son, Lord Caryll Molyneux (1626–99), the 3rd Viscount, had to lie low for a while on his family estate at Croxteth Hall. (This still stands to the east of Liverpool in the suburb of West Derby.)

However, tensions gradually eased so that, sometime around 1675, Lord Caryll felt confident enough to cut a track through the castle orchard. He named this Molyneux Lane and then Lord Molyneux Street (now Lord Street), and he built a town house on the north side of his new street. This was demolished in the nineteenth century and a Tesco store now stands on the site.

Molyneux's road led to the shore of a wide creek that needed a rowing boat to cross and which formed the eastern boundary of what was then still quite a small town. Liverpool townsfolk grumbled at this arrogance a little, but he was lord of the manor so most people kept their opinions about his new road to themselves.

Then, in 1669, Molyneux built a bridge linking his road and castle lands to the other side of the creek. However, this territory was nothing more than a vast area of very sparsely populated open land known as the Great Heath (or Great Waste). It stretched for miles and reached as far as the independent communities of Kensington, Edge Hill, Old

Swan, Wavertree, and Childwall. The creek still runs from the hills above Liverpool and down to the river, but today it is culverted completely and runs beneath many modern roads, including Whitechapel and Paradise Streets in the city centre.

Molyneux wanted to develop this section of the heath for his own commercial advantage, extending his holdings up the hill to what would eventually become Bold Street. But this, quite literally, was 'a bridge too far' for the townspeople. They felt that it was common land and belonged to them – once again, the Molyneux family were getting on the wrong side of the people! They also feared that Molyneux was trying to make a claim for all the lands of the heath, so they were not pleased.

Two local townsmen, Edward Marsh and James Whitfield, supported by their fellow citizens, promptly demolished Molyneux's bridge almost as soon as he built it. Molyneux had them imprisoned, but they were immediately bailed out by their friends, who also paid for solicitors to take up their case.

After a court hearing and protracted negotiations, and in return for permission to build his bridge, on 20 March 1672, Molyneux settled out of court. He agreed to sub-lease the lordship of the manor of Liverpool to the Town Corporation. This was to be for a period of 1,000 years and at an annual rent of £30, so it was a bargain. Molyneux also agreed that the townspeople of Liverpool should have title to the town land and its income, as well as having free access to the common land across his bridge.

The new bridge now indeed opened up new areas of land – and not only for Molyneux. By 1705, houses and businesses had begun to appear on new streets. Soon, the main thoroughfare of Church Street was laid out, and this meant that the town of Liverpool could now begin to grow.

In 1777, Lord Charles Molyneux (1748–95), 1st Earl of Sefton, was in dire need of cash. He was forced by circumstances to sell the lordship to two merchant speculators from London, for the sum of £2,250. This was clearly in breach of the lease agreement that the earl had with the town, but the people had no real authority to oppose one of Britain's leading aristocrats. There was no guarantee that the courts would support them this time, as the political power in the country had now shifted away from the ordinary people.

So Liverpudlians did the only thing possible. Representatives of the Corporation of Liverpool immediately followed the merchants, caught up with them, and persuaded (!?) the men to sell the manor back to them. Liverpool City Council still holds the manorial rights to the city today, but under licence from the monarch.

In 1715, Liverpool and the world's first commercial enclosed wet dock was opened (London's first dock was not opened until 1802). This eventually became known as the Old Dock, as the extent of Liverpool's docklands – and consequent world dominance in maritime trades – expanded steadily over the next 300 years. It was at this time that the creek was culverted and built over. Lord Molyneux's bridge was also built over in the process.

Centuries later, in the 1950s, the building that now houses McDonald's burger restaurant was being constructed at the corner of Paradise Street and Lord Street. This was to replace buildings that had been destroyed by German bombs during the Second World War. As excavations for new foundations were under way, some timbers from Lord Molyneux's bridge were discovered. They are still there, buried beneath the bustling crossroads of Holy Corner – the junction of Whitechapel, Church Street, Paradise Street, and Lord Street.

Lord Molyneux's bridge, discovered during post-war excavations. (Discover Liverpool library)

7

ℌale ℌead and the ℒighthouse

The ancient township of Hale sits comfortably a mile or two beyond the southern boundaries of Liverpool. Hale was awarded its royal charter as a township by King John (1166–1216) in November 1203. This was four years before its neighbour, Liverpool, received its own charter from the same monarch in August 1207. The village is a delightful place, with thatched cottages, welcoming pubs, and a graceful manor house. It had a famous resident, a 'giant' named John Middleton, known also as the Childe of Hale (1578–1623). John's tale is told in my first volume of *Merseyside Tales*.

From the eighteenth century, the freemen of Hale were allowed to elect their own lord mayor – a very special privilege indeed – and this tradition continues. Today, however, the freemen of Hale are local people who have a record of service to the community. Likewise, the mayor, who serves a three-year term, is elected on the basis of civic and community involvement. At mayoral election time, the investitures take place in the village, and sometimes in the Childe of Hale Pub or the Wellington Pub.

The independence of Hale and its community, as well as its somewhat 'backwater' location, saved the township from the encroachments of Liverpool, and enabled it to preserve and strengthen its own identity. Nevertheless, administratively, modern Hale is not part of the City of Liverpool, nor is it officially in Merseyside. Nominally, the township falls under the jurisdiction of the Metropolitan Borough of Halton, which is in the county of Cheshire. However, Hale has always been a manorial possession, and the entire township and most of its lands are still in private hands; although the rights and privileges of the lord of the manor have long since been eroded.

Hale nestles directly on the banks of the River Mersey and if one strolls from the centre of the village, along Church Road and past St Mary's Church (where the Childe of Hale lies buried), the road becomes a delightful walk out to a small promontory of rock. This is named Hale Head, and there is a tiny beach of sand and sandstone, called the Red Rocks. From this point, there are stunning views across the Mersey Basin, looking towards the towns of Widnes and Runcorn and the hills of Frodsham and Helsby. Ships passing along the Manchester Ship Canal and the dramatic road and rail bridges that span this part of the river all add to the impressive scene.

On the very end of the promontory stands Hale Lighthouse with its keeper's cottage. It was built in 1906 to replace a previous light set on top of a shorter stack that had been erected in 1838. The current stack is 45ft (13.7m) tall and its static white beam once shone across the Mersey Basin at a height of 70ft (21.3m) above sea level.

The lamp was lit by oil and its large and sophisticated reflector meant that the beam could be seen over 40 miles away. This was very important as this is the widest point of the River Mersey, and the light served a very useful purpose for vessels on the once-crowded stretch of the great waterway. It warned them of the dangers of Hale Head and its surrounding shallow shoals and treacherous rocks.

The light was kept lit throughout the Second World War, although this did attract an enemy aircraft on one occasion and bombs were dropped nearby. Fortunately, the lighthouse escaped damage, although the keeper's wife was machine-gunned by another passing Nazi plane as she mistakenly opened the shutters on the windows of the cottage. By sheer luck, she was not hit.

In 1958, the decision was taken to finally turn off the light. There was no longer much shipping at this end of the river so the lighthouse had become redundant. All the building's equipment was removed, but the lenses for the light can now be seen in the Merseyside Maritime Museum, at the Royal Albert Dock in Liverpool. The lighthouse, its cottage and surrounding land, were then sold as a private residence and it has remained so ever since. As such, it is not open to the public, but the footpath that is part of the Mersey Way and the nature reserve passes alongside the structure, giving visitors an excellent view of the old building.

8

ZEPPELINS OVER WIDNES AND HALTON HEROES

During the First World War, large numbers of men from Runcorn and Widnes served with the armed forces. Many fought and died. Most of the factories in the area contributed significantly to the production of goods and munitions for the war effort, so some local men were in reserved occupations during the conflict. Older children, too, worked in the munitions factories. However, large numbers of local women played an often-overlooked role in working for the war effort against the Germans, and it is important to acknowledge and remember their contribution.

Although the First World War was mostly fought on the Continent, in 1918 two bombs were dropped on Widnes by a German Zeppelin air balloon. Both bombs fell in the area of Bold and luckily there were no casualties. Today, there is a damaged milestone with a plaque in Victoria Park, Widnes, commemorating the attack.

During this dreadful war, both Runcorn and Widnes produced soldiers who were recognised for their bravery. Private Thomas 'Todger' Alfred Jones (1880–1956), from Runcorn, was presented with the Victoria Cross by King George V in 1916. This was awarded for bravery in the face of enemy fire and for single-handedly capturing over 100 German soldiers.

Also awarded the Victoria Cross was Flight Sergeant Thomas Mottershead (1892–1917), of the Royal Flying Corps, who had been born in Widnes. Following an attack by two German aircraft over Belgium, and having been badly burnt, Sergeant Mottershead managed to return his aircraft to Allied lines, saving the life of his passenger. Tragically, he died from his injuries five days later and was awarded his medal posthumously.

And finally, Commander Thomas Wilkinson (1898–1942) of the Royal Navy, from West Bank, Widnes, was awarded the Victoria Cross in 1942. Sadly, this medal was also presented posthumously, following the sinking of Commander Wilkinson's ship in East Asia. It was awarded for inflicting significant damage on a Japanese naval force despite being heavily outnumbered.

In March 1941, a German aircraft was shot down over Widnes and landed on Leigh recreation ground. The three surviving members of crew were captured.

On South Lane in Bold there was a POW camp built to house Italian prisoners of war, many of whom worked as labourers on local farms.

Often overlooked in history, it is important to remember that every town and village in Britain has some story to tell; some significance in our long history; or some hero or heroine to remember and honour – and Widnes and Runcorn are no exceptions!

The Halton Heroes memorial. (Discover Liverpool library)

9

ᚦHE ᚨRCHWAY ᚱOAD ᚢIKINGS

The River Alt was once one of the most significant waterways on Merseyside and it virtually encircles the city of Liverpool. The Alt rises in a marshy field, known as Hag Plantation, which lies to the south of Huyton Lane on the edge of Huyton town centre. The field was once part of a much larger wetland area but most of this has been drained and built upon. One of the most recent developments is a small housing estate off Huyton Lane, known as Marshfield Close.

The River Alt was much wider 1,000 years ago and the Vikings sailed upon it. In fact, they gave names to many places in and around Merseyside, including Roby, Skelmersdale, Aigburth, Irby, Croxteth, Toxteth, Kirkby, Heswall, and Thingwall. The name of Huyton itself is actually Anglo-Saxon, so predates the Vikings. A huge lake existed in Huyton, in those times, where the Hag Plantation now stretches. Sand has also been found beneath Huyton itself, confirming that this was likely to have been a landing place for ships in ancient times.

From Huyton the river next runs through Croxteth Park, then roughly follows the M57 south of Kirkby, and flows north of Aintree and south of Maghull. It finally runs south of Formby and empties into the Irish Sea, near the edge of the River Mersey estuary at Hightown.

We know that in the early AD 900s, Vikings who had previously invaded Ireland sailed from there across to the Isle of Man, Wales, and to Wirral and what would eventually become Liverpool and Merseyside. Marauding across the territory on a rampage of rape and pillage, eventually they calmed down and many settled in the region. They sailed the local rivers, including the Alt, to explore the hinterland of the north-west.

Here, they found the territory to be fertile and rich in resources, not least of all arable land, livestock, and fish. Some of the Norse

A Viking longship. (Discover Liverpool library)

immigrants married into the local population and raised families, whilst others created new farmsteads and communities. From bloodthirsty warriors they evolved into hunter-gatherers and farmers, and also entered into trade and commerce.

But now we come to more recent times – in fact, to the Victorian era. This saw many great technological innovations, and not least of these, of course, were the railways. Indeed, the first, intercity passenger railway in the world was built in the 1820s, to connect Liverpool with Manchester using new steam locomotives.

The sweat and back-breaking labour of thousands of workmen, known as 'navvies' and using mainly picks and shovels, constructed this stunning engineering achievement. This included digging cuttings and tunnels through hills and high ground, as well as building high embankments and sixty-three viaducts and bridges across lowlands and valleys. Many deep hollows also had to be filled in.

According to newspaper reports at the time, as part of this work on the new line in 1828, navvies were building a bridge for the railway across one of the roads leading into Huyton. As they were digging, they discovered the remains of a Viking longship lying buried deep in the sand and shale below the earth topsoil. This proved that the course of the Alt had once run through this part of the district and, at that time, had been wide enough to allow ships like this to navigate their way inland. However, why the vessel had been left abandoned here, no one could tell, and this remains a mystery today.

Because of the new bridge, the road was renamed Archway Road, which it is still known as today, but there remains another mystery. What happened to the excavated longship?

It is not in any local museum or collection that I can discover, nor is it in the World Museum on William Brown Street, or in the Museum of Liverpool at the Pier Head. Perhaps the navvies simply left it where they found it and re-covered it over with earth. Perhaps it lies there still, under the modern, tarmacked roadway. Wherever it is, the next time you drive under the bridge at Archway Road, spare a thought for the Viking warriors who became the new citizens of Huyton over a millennium ago: perhaps an ancestor of your own was one of these remarkable people!

10

𝕿HE 𝕭IDSTON AND 𝕿RANMERE 𝕭UNKERS

During the Second World War and following the catastrophic German bombing raids of 1941, which devastated Liverpool, Wirral, and Bootle, Wirral's Civil Defence Emergency Committee was granted unprecedented funds by the government. This was to establish two networks of deep, underground air-raid shelters. One of these sprawled under Tranmere, around Olive Mount, Thompson Street, and Holborn Hill. The other was dug out under Bidston Hill's Rhododendron Garden, with its entrance facing Hoylake Road. These all still exist.

Special permit vouchers were issued to local residents to guarantee them places in the shelters, as work to excavate the tunnels went on. By

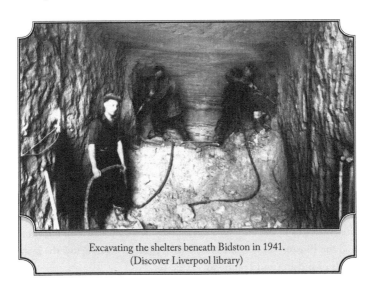

Excavating the shelters beneath Bidston in 1941.
(Discover Liverpool library)

June 1943, the work was finished and had cost £163,000. Birkenhead Corporation paid £48,006 of this amount.

The work was plagued with trespassers and vandalism, so this is not just a modern problem! Around 950 tons of sand were excavated from under Bidston Hill and then sold to a local contractor for building purposes. The rest of the spoil was tipped close to the entrance, which is why there is such an area of high, grassed embankments around the Hoylake Road/Fender Lane area.

The Bidston shelters are 7ft (2.1m) wide and 6ft (1.8m) high, with large, barrel-vaulted roofs. There were 2,213 bunks and 793 seats, as well as a canteen, staff dormitory, toilets, washing facilities, medical posts, and a ventilation shaft that could double as an emergency escape hatch if necessary.

Although the tunnels never saw the scale of use they were intended for, residents' vouchers still survive and people did shelter under Bidston.

At the outbreak of the war the British Government also instructed Birkenhead Corporation to excavate and build what would be the most expensive, underground air-raid shelter in the country beneath the Holborn Hill area. This was specifically to protect the workers at the nearby Cammell Laird shipyards – vital to the war effort.

This network of deep bunkers covered a distance of 6,500ft (1.9km) and cost an estimated £129,000. The shelters had beds and bunks for over 6,000 people, including children. Also incorporated were lavatories, a medical wing, a canteen, and even a library.

The Tranmere tunnels were stripped of all their fixtures and fittings after the war, and it is believed that the lavatories were removed and then installed in houses that were then being built on the new Woodchurch Estate. From 1948, the Tranmere shelters were used for storage by the Ministry of Food.

At the height of the Cold War, when a nuclear attack was expected at any time by Russia, it was planned that the Tranmere shelters should be used if necessary. This remained the case from 1947 to 1956, and it was planned that around 4,160 people could shelter there. In the 1980s the entrances to the underground bunkers were all sealed up but they, and the Bidston tunnels, are all still there, 80ft (24.4m) below the busy roads of Bidston and Tranmere.

11

𝕿he 𝕵ron 𝕸en: 𝕱acing 𝕿he 𝕱uture 𝕴n 𝕿he 𝕾hadow of 𝕿he 𝕻ast

Just to the north of Liverpool are the coastal districts of Waterloo and Blundellsands, and the town of Crosby. The latter stands on the shore overlooking the estuary of the Mersey and out to Liverpool Bay. The seaside town's extensive area of beach and sandhills are a popular recreation destination for people from the whole district and from Liverpool.

However, a particularly special feature of this section of waterfront are the 100 cast-iron sculptures of naked men who stand at various points on the shore, gazing out to sea in full-frontal imperturbability. Designed and created by the artist Anthony Gormley (b.1950) and titled *Another Place*, they are spread over 2 miles of sand between Waterloo and Blundellsands.

The figures are cast reproductions of the artist's body and are each just over 6ft (1.8m) tall. As the tides ebb and flow, they are repeatedly submerged and then revealed again by the sea. First exhibited here in 1997, and permanently sited from 2007, the figures are designed to explore man's relationship with nature, Anthony says:

> Here, at the edge of the sea, time is tested by tide; architecture by the elements; and the prevalence of sky seems to question the earth's substance.
>
> In this work human life is tested against planetary time. This sculpture exposes to light and time the nakedness of a particular and peculiar body. It is no hero, no ideal, just the industrially reproduced body of a

The Iron Men at Crosby Shore. (Image by Dennis Turner)

middle-aged man trying to remain standing and trying to breathe, facing a horizon busy with ships moving materials and manufactured things around the planet.

The iron men seem also to reflect the typically independent fortitude of Liverpudlians and Merseysiders. They also represent our capacity to survive and sustain, to fight against the odds and go on despite the most apparently impossible circumstances.

Elsewhere on the Crosby foreshore can be found some bitter reminders of the devastation caused to Bootle and Liverpool by German bombers, during the May Blitz of 1941. Victorian roads that connect with twentieth-century highways still lead to lanes that take you down to the shore of the River Mersey. Here, the waters of the Mersey Estuary wash over bomb-blasted remnants of these Nazi attacks, which tell their tale of fire and explosion, terror and injury, and death and dreadful destruction.

For here, at Crosby, are stone fragments, both large and small, of walls, doorways, roofs, chimneys, portals, arches, and windows. These are from long-gone buildings, in what was the most heavily bombed city and port in Britain (outside London) during the Second World War. In sheer tonnage of incendiary and high-explosive bombs, nowhere took more than Liverpool, Bootle, Wallasey and Birkenhead.

After the fall of France in 1940, and before America came into the war in December 1941, apart from the support we had from Canada and the colonies of the British Empire, Britain stood completely alone against the Nazi juggernaut that had rolled out across Europe. Liverpool and Merseyside were vital to the nation's survival, as it was through the port and the waterfront on both sides of the Mersey that the convoys of ships to and from America, the Empire and, in due course, from Russia, brought food, tools, fuel, medicines, munitions, and other supplies to beleaguered Britain.

Hitler was perfectly well aware of our strategic position, and he launched the relentless U-boat attacks on the convoys that became known as the Battle of the Atlantic. This was the longest-running campaign of the war because it lasted for the entire duration of the conflict.

Because of the port's strategic importance, Hitler was determined to completely obliterate Liverpool and the towns and communities of Wirral, so he ordered Hermann Goering's Luftwaffe to 'bomb them into oblivion'. The first of dozens of air raids took place in the autumn of 1940, and the first German bombs landed on Merseyside on 9 August 1940, at Prenton in Birkenhead.

The bombing continued intermittently until, just before Christmas 1940, there came three nights of mass raids. These resulted in great gaps in the streets of Liverpool and Wirral, and much loss of life. Nevertheless, the most violent aerial assault, the real Blitz, was launched against the city during the nights of 1–8 May 1941. This would be the worst week of sustained raids on any part of Britain, including the capital, and was an all-or-nothing attempt by the Germans to wreck the port from which the Western Approaches were being defended. After this, the Nazis continued to bomb Liverpool and Wirral almost every night during the remainder of May and the first two weeks of June.

Altogether, there were seventy-nine separate Liverpool air raids during the Blitz, and it was estimated that out of the almost 300,000 homes in Liverpool at that time, around 200,000 were damaged and 11,000 destroyed. Indeed, throughout the city and its suburbs, there

The remnants of the bombed buildings during the May
Blitz of 1941. (Discover Liverpool library)

were 15,000 blitzed sites. There was much loss of life and, between July
1940 and January 1942, the Luftwaffe bombing raids on Liverpool and
Merseyside killed:

2,716 people in Liverpool,
442 people in Birkenhead,
409 people in Bootle, and
332 people in Wallasey –
and injured more than 10,000

Each stone and brick remnant of the Blitz at Crosby is slowly sinking
over the decades. Eventually, they will all be lost beneath the sands and
shingles as the waves wash tide and time over them. But the people
of Liverpool, Wirral, Bootle, Crosby, and the other townships and
communities to the north of the great city on the Mersey will go on,
like the iron men. Together, we are facing boldly towards the rest of the
world and towards the future, but the memory of those dark days will
live long in the hearts, minds, and communities of the people of this
part of north-west Britain.

12

A Memorial in Time: The Sarah Pooley Clocktower

At the heart of the once independent and very ancient village of Wavertree, now nestled in the southern suburbs of Liverpool, is a busy traffic roundabout. On this can be found a former waiting room for the trams that used to run through here. Standing next to this structure is a tall, impressive, late-Victorian clocktower, generally referred to as the Picton Clock.

The clock was named after Sir James Allanson Picton (1832–89), who was a resident of Wavertree. Picton was locally and nationally renowned as a historian, author, and architect, who designed many buildings in and around Liverpool. These included Holy Trinity Church, Hoylake; the original Liverpool Corn Exchange on Fenwick Street; the original Tower Building on Water Street; the Temple on Dale Street; and the Hargreaves Building (the former Racquets Club) on Chapel Street. He also designed part of the Central Libraries on William Brown Street, and the Picton Reading Room is named after him.

In 1847, Picton constructed a grand house for himself, built in local red sandstone. He named this Sandy Knowe and it still stands at the top of Olive Mount. This is now a nursing home, and is the highest point in Wavertree village, standing at 215ft (65.5m) above sea level.

Knighted by Queen Victoria in 1881, Sir James was a much-respected individual in his home village as well as in Liverpool, and he was a great benefactor to both places. Picton was supported in all he did by his devoted wife, Sarah, with whom he was deeply in love, and whose maiden name had been Pooley. Tragically though, in 1879, and after fifty years of very happy marriage, Sarah died. James was bereft and, as a memorial to his wife, he designed and built the clocktower in the village. It was officially named the Sarah Pooley Clocktower and was formally unveiled in 1884. The large memorial bears a number of embellishments and inscriptions, the most meaningful of which reads, 'Time wasted is existence; used is life'.

The Sarah Pooley Memorial Clock in Wavertree village. (Discover Liverpool library)

'ROAST BEEF' AND OTHER CROSBY RELICS

I make no apologies for returning to Crosby for my next stories. It is just that there is so much to tell about the history of this small but important and fascinating little town.

In fact, I will begin with the most ancient relic to be found here, a 20-ton Ice Age boulder known as the Crosby Stone. During the Ice Age, which began around 2.5 million years ago and lasted until around 12,000 years ago, this great rock was carried down to the area from the Lake District by a glacier.

It stood in the centre of the town for many years until, in 1926, it was relocated to local Coronation Park as an important and revered

Prehistoric fossilised footprints at Formby. (Discover Liverpool library)

local artefact. Sadly though, in May 2013, it was severely damaged by local vandals and so is now even more protected and revered by the more stable majority of Crosby residents.

But there are ancient human relics in the area, too. Indeed, prehistoric human footprints have been seen on the beach at Formby for a very long time. Recent high tides and stormy conditions on the Mersey have now revealed some on Crosby shore too. These prints can be seen as two parallel sets of tracks running for a length of around 16½ft (5m). They are believed to have been made by three people, probably male, who each stood at around 6ft (1.8m) tall. The fossilised footprints probably date from around 4,000 to 6,000 years ago. What look like cattle hoof marks and tracks of other animals and birds have also been exposed on our local, north-western coastlines, and a monitoring process is now in place, keeping a lookout for even more ancient prints.

However, perhaps of equal curiosity value was the local living relic, the Crosby hermit.

Whether Jack Johnson was born in Crosby or somewhere else entirely is not certain, but it is known that he was born in 1829. What has also been discovered is that his years as a young man at least were adventurous. He was a soldier, who fought in the Crimean War, which lasted from 1853 to 1856. After this, he became a seaman,

The Crosby Stone, which is now in Coronation Park. (Discover Liverpool library)

sailing between Liverpool and New Orleans on ships bringing cotton into England.

Around 1871, Jack gave up his life on the ocean wave for one on land as a gamekeeper. He was watching over game fowl on Crosby

Marshes, probably for the local, wealthy Blundell family. Here, he built a ramshackle hut for himself out of planks, sailcloth, and driftwood, and he made the marshland his permanent home.

Jack's hut stood on the beach at the end of what is now Hall Road, and he kept himself to himself, seldom talking to anyone and not usually welcoming visitors. He became an almost total recluse and was soon known locally as the Hermit of the Sandhills. His life at war

Jack Johnson, or 'Roast Beef', the Crosby Hermit. (Discover Liverpool library)

and at sea, as well as on the often harsh and bleak marshes, had given him weather-beaten features and a ruddy complexion, so he was also known as 'Roast Beef'!

Jack supplemented his meagre income by catching and selling fish and shellfish, and he largely lived on gifts of food left for him by local people. These kind folk did not simply give him scraps or leftovers, but actually took turns in cooking meals for him, so he was clearly liked by the community as well as being well cared for by them.

At some point earlier in his life Jack had married and had a son. What became of his wife is unknown, and the only thing that is known of his son is that, in 1902, he fought at the Siege of Ladysmith during the Boer War. It is also uncertain when Jack died, although it was sometime in the 1920s. He was buried in a local pauper's grave, unmarked and unknown, but at least not forgotten.

𝕿HE 𝕻EOPLE'S 𝕻ARLIAMENT AND THE 𝕻EOPLE'S 𝕮LUB

Spellow Lane in Walton was once an ancient and important trackway. Today, it runs from County Road, up a flank of Walton Hill, to where Everton Football Club had its original home at Goodison Park. During Anglo-Saxon times, from around AD 410, the site of the football ground was actually the location of an ancient chieftain's burial mound, or tumulus. There were a number of such places in and around Liverpool, where local leaders were laid to rest with great ceremony: But these, of course, have long since disappeared.

'Spel-low' translates from the Anglo-Saxon as 'Speech-Hill', showing that this was also a Parliamentary, law-making, or tribal governance meeting place. This was where important community and legal decisions were taken, using an early form of democracy. It is also likely that, from the time when the Vikings invaded what would become Liverpool, around the early ninth century, they also settled their differences at the top of Spellow Hill.

Around 1270, a windmill was built on the hill, which soon became very important, because local people came here from all around the district to have their corn ground into flour. The ancient mill burnt down in 1828.

In the late thirteenth century, a grand house was built nearby by a man named Thomas Spellow, so he was clearly a local! His property consisted of the main house with a number of large outbuildings and a chapel. (It also had numerous hiding places that were used by priests during the religious troubles of the seventeenth century.)

In 1426 though, this entire area, including Walton and Fazakerley, became the property and estate of the important, Norman, Fazakerley family, who gave their name to that district of Liverpool. They also owned the manor of Old Swan, and their coat of arms bears three swans. This is how that district got its name.

But what of Everton FC's connection with Speech Hill?

Everton Football Club was founded in 1878 by the Reverend Ben Swift Chambers (1845–1901). He was minister of the St Domingo Methodist Chapel in nearby Everton Village. In 1892 though, there was a major disagreement within the leadership, management, players, and membership of the club. There was a split, and a breakaway team was formed who named themselves Liverpool Football Club. They remained at what had been the Everton club's original ground at Anfield, and this remains Liverpool FC's ground today.

However, the original Everton FC now had to find a new home. The land at the top of Spellow Lane – Speech Hill – was then in private ownership and known as the Mere Field. The owner donated the land to the football club, but the problem was that it was uneven, full of weeds, nettles, and crab-grass, and was completely strewn with large rocks and small boulders.

Everton's first stadium at Goodison Park, previously the Mere Field. (Liverpool Athenaeum library)

The club's players, managers, supporters, and members of the public worked long and hard to completely clear the ground by hand. They did so until it was flat, even, and suitable for use as a football pitch. It was because of this undertaking by local people that Everton FC has ever since been known as the People's Club.

The club then set about building Britain's first, purpose-built football stadium, Goodison Park, at a cost of £3,000. They built two uncovered stands and one covered stand for spectators at an additional total cost of £1,400.

In due course, Everton FC outgrew Goodison Park and Speech Hill, and at the time of writing is in the process of moving into a state-of-the-art, 52,000-seat football, sports, and events stadium built over Liverpool's Bramley-Moore Dock. The cost of this is something in the region of £500 million.

15

𝕿𝕳𝕰 𝕷𝕴𝕿𝕿𝕷𝕰 𝕿𝕽𝕬𝕸𝕻

This story begins with the birth of a boy named Charles in April 1889, in London, to Hannah and Charles Snr. They were a married couple of touring vaudeville entertainers. However, mother and son, and his older half-brother, were soon abandoned by Charles Snr, who was an alcoholic. They suffered such hardship that the boys twice spent time in the workhouse, even before Charles reached 9 years of age.

Even so, their mother was loving, and always tried to keep her boys happy and entertained. This was despite her recurring mental illness and resulting periods in mental asylums.

In 1900, at the aged of 11, Charles, who had some talent as a singer and dancer, joined a touring clog-dancing troupe, known as the Eight Lancashire Lads. The boy now left home and went on the road around Britain with the troupe. His father died the following year.

The clog dancers were highly successful and popular, appearing in music halls and theatres around Britain, but especially in the north-west of England. They performed regularly at the Argyle Theatre in Birkenhead and at Hengler's Circus in Liverpool. This latter theatre went on to become the famous Hippodrome Theatre and was later converted into a cinema of the same name.

While appearing for a long engagement at Hengler's, Charles stayed in digs in nearby Salisbury Street in Everton. As he was still of school age, the young boy was required to register and attend the school nearest to where he was staying. This was the Jesuit-run Roman Catholic school of Saint Francis Xavier, also in Salisbury Street.

The school buildings still stand today but are now the Everton Campus of Liverpool Hope University. In later life, Charles would say that, of all the schools he attended during his complex and demanding early life, he never felt more welcomed or cared for than he did during the few weeks he spent in Liverpool, at SFX. This is to the credit of his fellow pupils, and the priests and staff at the school, and to the people of Liverpool, particularly because the boy was Jewish.

The youngster's talent had certainly developed by now and he had become a truly gifted dancer, acrobat, and clown. He soon became extremely popular in his own right. In 1910, aged 17, he joined Fred Karno's Circus. This was a famous touring music-hall and comedy troupe, where Charles was also a great success. The troupe then went on tour in America, where, in 1912, at the age of 23, he was

Charles, aged 19. (Liverpool Athenaeum library)

talent-spotted by Mack Sennett (1880-1960), the renowned film producer, director, and comic actor. He now joined the Sennett studios to appear in the silent films *The Keystone Comedies*.

So, have you worked out who this talented young man was yet? He was, of course, Charlie Chaplin.

His salary, in only a few years, rose from $500 to $10,000 a week. He was also paid a $150,000 annual bonus based on sales, which were phenomenal and global. Between 1912 and 1919, Charlie Chaplin made sixty short silent films and had invented his unique comedy character and persona, which he named 'The Little Tramp'. He had now also become world famous.

It was in 1919 that he formed a partnership with three other famous and successful Hollywood personalities: Mary Pickford (1892–1979); D.W. Griffith (1875–1948); and Douglas Fairbanks Senior (1883–1939). Together, they created the United Artists film production and distribution company in an effort to gain greater control of how their films were made and shown.

Charlie Chaplin was knighted in 1975 by Queen Elizabeth II (1926-2022), and died in 1977, at the age of 88. So, the young boy who spent a brief but happy time in school in Liverpool, went on to become arguably the greatest, most world-renowned and popular comedy entertainer of the first half of the twentieth century. He has left behind him a great legacy and, who knows, perhaps Liverpool played a small part in this.

16

THE MUSEUM OF ANATOMY

Now for the story of one of Liverpool's most popular attractions and one that drew curious crowds for almost 100 years in the city – the Liverpool Museum of Anatomy.

Joseph Thornton Woodhead was born in Halifax, Yorkshire, in 1816. As a young man seeking adventure, he travelled to Dresden in Germany. Here, he became a physician and learned the difficult art of anatomical wax modelling. He was very skilful and accurate, and was soon being commissioned to make anatomical models for museums and medical galleries all over Europe.

In due course, Joseph found himself touring America with his own travelling exhibition of wax models and drawings of human organs and body parts. All went well until he arrived in New York, where angry Puritan residents in the city called his exhibition 'sexual slapdashery and wanton obscenity'. In 1850, he was driven out and fled via Dublin to Liverpool to change his fortunes.

Joseph found temporary premises on Lime Street in the town centre, where he opened his first Liverpool Museum of Anatomy. Here, to an eager and very curious paying public, he displayed around 750 grisly wax models of diseased organs, morbid deformities, and genitalia in a range of states of abnormality and infection.

As profits continued to grow, Joseph was soon able to move to more suitable premises at 29 Paradise Street. The number of his exhibits also grew and soon reached over 1,000 – all in 'living and livid colour'!

Specifically, there were models in wax of saints and sinners, plus a large tableaux of the fires of Hell. Other models, all actual size and biologically accurate, showed various forms of deformity, while others showed most of the internal organs. There were adult and child skeletons, and accurate displays of common surgical procedures,

The Museum of Anatomy on Paradise Street.
(Discover Liverpool library)

such as the removal of kidney stones. One model showed the digestive system and digestion, including 'articles of human food, and what they are converted into'.

However, the exhibits that attracted most attention were those of obstetrics, masturbation, circumcision, hermaphrodites, and 'freaks of nature'. Other displays were advertised as demonstrating 'the fruits of sin and the consequences of uncleanliness', including the symptoms of syphilis and gonorrhoea. As a result, queues to see this collection regularly stretched out into the street.

This was strictly an 'adults only' exhibition and, in keeping with the mores of the time, the anatomical exhibits were generally considered not to be salacious and, in fact, were regarded by many as being a completely socially acceptable form of educational entertainment.

The museum was open every day from 10 a.m. until 9 p.m., but only for gentlemen. Ladies were admitted, but only on Tuesdays and Fridays, from 2 p.m. to 5 p.m. Joseph defended the 'sexual liberality' of admitting females as being an important informational opportunity for women who cared for their families' health.

However, the museum did cause considerable offence and raised objections from some prominent dignitaries. So much so that, in 1874, Joseph Woodhead was prosecuted under the Obscene Publications Act. He was fined, but the Anatomical Museum did not close, as the displays did not exactly fall within the remit of the Act. In fact, the museum survived after Joseph's death and passed to his son-in-law.

In 1937, it was sold to a Liverpool merchant, Henry A. Holmes, who almost immediately closed it and sold the entire exhibition to Louis Tussaud (1869–1938). He was the great-grandson of the renowned portrait artist in wax, Madame Marie Tussaud (1761–1850), and he mounted the anatomical exhibits in a special curtained-off area above his large waxworks on Central Parade in Blackpool. He had opened this as a tourist attraction in 1929.

The display survived for many years and was a popular additional attraction in the waxworks. My parents kept me out of that display – and the Chamber of Horrors – during family outings to the resort when I was a young boy in the 1950s, much to my disgruntlement! So I compensated for this deprivation by making a point of visiting the waxworks, and the 'special section', on my own frequent trips to Blackpool with my friends during the 1960s, 1970s, and 1980s, after which time the novelty eventually wore off!!

Louis Tussaud's Waxworks was bought out by Blackpool Council who, in 2010, closed the entire attraction and sold it to the Merlin Entertainment Group. They refurbished the building and, in 2011, reopened it as Madame Tussauds Waxworks. However, by this time, the anatomical exhibits had vanished.

I have been in touch with Tussauds in an attempt to trace them, but whichever staff member I speak to, whenever I call, always denies any knowledge of intimate, anatomical, wax body parts! Perhaps the management are too embarrassed to admit that they once owned this bizarre collection. But they did!

So, no remnants seem to survive of Joseph Woodhead's handmade and sculpted wax anatomical exhibits, or of his Paradise Street Museum. These seem to have been firmly consigned to history – or to the secret museum of some unknown private collector.

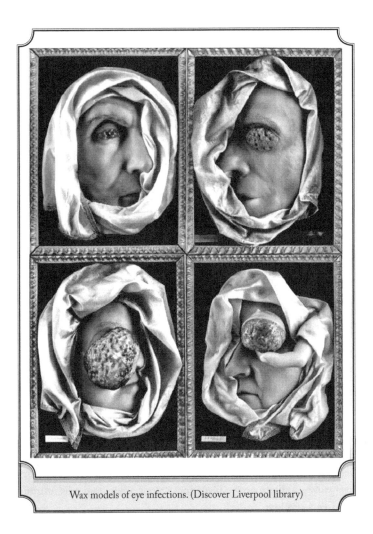

Wax models of eye infections. (Discover Liverpool library)

17

ᎢHE ᎻORRORS OF CRANK CAVERNS

There are almost as many fascinating and unusual stories about subterranean Merseyside as there are above ground. The whole region is riddled with caverns and caves, tunnels and passageways. Many of these are man-made as well as natural, and quite a few combine both, including mysterious Crank Caverns.

These are a complex network of caves and tunnels stretching for some distance near Crank, just outside St Helens, and are what remains of the Rainford Delph Quarry. There are many tales associated with this creepy place, located as it is in dense and equally eerie woodland.

Records state that 'sandstone quarrying' began here as early as 1730, but it was actually mined rather than quarried, along many different seams of stone. This is why there are a number of passageways that twist and wind for varied distances and at different depths.

Reports tell that the caverns were listed as a colliery by 1854, although no coal was mined here, of course. It also appears that they were still being worked early into the twentieth century. When work ceased, the caves and all the surrounding woodlands were used as a game reserve by John Stanley (1918–94), the 18th Earl of Derby, who owned all the surrounding land.

Then the Second World War broke out, so the caverns were taken over by the War Office and used as an ammunition store for the Anti-Aircraft Battery at Crank. After the war, and with no further use being found for them, even by Lord Derby, they were left to become overgrown, and are now a place for curious adults and adventurous children to explore.

The entrance to Crank Caverns. (Discover Liverpool library)

There are, in fact, two sets of caverns. The first has seven excavated entrance portals that all lead down to a broad cave. The second set is found at the bottom of a nearby deep ditch. Here, there are two tunnels, one quite short and another leading into a deeper set of caves. There is no firm evidence that caves or tunnels existed before the early eighteenth century, so it seems that they exist only because of the mining operations from that time.

Although the entrances and tunnels are man-made, they do appear to connect with deeper natural caverns, and there are all kinds of stories associated with these. One states that during the Protestant Reformation, local Catholics being persecuted by King Henry VIII (1491–1547) took shelter in the caverns and held secret masses here.

Other legends say that some of the tunnels lead to various places in the area, including to Up Holland, near Skelmersdale, as well as to various places in St Helens. One of the most popular local legends is that one tunnel leads from a cave all the way to beneath St Helens Town Hall. It is said that this was used to drag unfortunate criminals (and others) from the town to the caverns in secret, so that they could be hanged below ground and out of the sight and knowledge of the people.

Of course, there is also the tale of the Troglodyte Dwarves, who were once believed to inhabit another network of deep caves nearby. Whether or not these were connected to Crank Caverns is unclear, but in the eighteenth century, a small group of children decided to explore these particular caves. They wanted to discover if the stories they had heard about the strange little men who lived deep underground were true. They got more than they bargained for.

Four children went into the caves but only one of them ever came back out again. When he emerged, he was in a dreadful state of shock, with his clothes mostly torn off and his body scratched and scraped all over. He told how he had only barely managed to escape the hungry grasps of 'vicious little old men'. He described them clearly as having long, matted, filthy grey hair and beards, and equally long, talon-like fingernails. They had killed his friends and then chased after him but, fortunately, he had escaped their clutches.

This was apparently not the first such incident, so the authorities sent two heavily armed soldiers into the caverns. Although they never saw, let alone captured, any 'vicious dwarves', they did report finding a large heap of human bones. They also found a child's head in one of the caves, along with evidence of cannibalism.

Most disturbingly, they had also discovered the ruins of an ancient church or temple of an unknown denomination. Its interior was lit by three large candles and grotesque gargoyles formed part of an altar, casting huge, shifting shadows in the guttering candlelight. They also reported that, as they were searching the warren of caves and tunnels they felt as if they were being watched, and they also heard low voices, muttering in a strange language.

A second investigation was ordered and, soon afterwards, gunpowder was used to blast the caves into collapse and to seal them shut. But, while the dwarves' caves are now buried forever, the Crank Caverns remain.

Could there be a subterranean passage, yet to be unearthed, that would lead back to them? If so, would anyone really want to go exploring any newly discovered Crank Caverns for fear of what, or who, might be revealed?

18

THE PETRIFIED PRIEST OF TUE BROOK HOUSE

In the Liverpool district of Tuebrook, on a road named Mill Bank that leads from Muirhead Avenue to Queens Drive, stands Tue Brook House. This is the second-oldest, continually occupied house in Liverpool, and the ancient Tue Brook runs underneath the old building.

The brook was given its name by Viking invaders. They settled here around 1,000 years ago and established a community. All trace of the now culverted brook in the district has vanished, except for its name, although it does occasionally break ground elsewhere in the city suburbs.

Tue Brook House was built in 1615, by a wealthy yeoman farmer named John Mercer, for himself and his family. It has two floors, oak beams, mullioned windows, and two side wings. A datestone is set in the lintel above the front door, which also bears the initials 'JM'.

John Mercer was a Roman Catholic, and during those days, it was against the law to be a Catholic or to have Catholic services anywhere. People had to hold their services and prayers in secret, in houses like John's. Priests would come, in secret and in disguise, to lead the services. They had to keep a lookout for Puritan soldiers though, who might come and arrest, jail, torture, or even execute all of them, but especially the priest.

When he was holding a secret mass for his Catholic family, friends, and neighbours, John Mercer placed one of his servants in an upstairs room to keep a lookout through the window. If soldiers were sighted approaching the farm then a warning was shouted down the stairs. This was so that Bibles and prayer books could be hidden in a secret hole beneath one of the stone slabs that made up the floor. But, they also had to hide the priest!

There were two fireplaces inside the house, and between the two chimneys was a tiny, secret room known as a priest hole. John had built this into his house for times of danger.

On one occasion, just as the people inside had managed to hide the priest from view, soldiers rode up to the door of John Mercer's farmhouse and marched straight in. They ransacked the place, looking for Bibles, prayer books, and for the priest. He was crammed in his tiny, secret hiding place, absolutely terrified out of his wits! Fortunately, the soldiers found nothing, so John and his Catholic family and friends had escaped arrest and torture.

Once the puritan troops had gone, and the servant on lookout had confirmed this, John and his friends went to let the cleric out of his hiding place. Tragically, they found that the poor man had died of fright.

During the Victorian period, Tue Brook House became the home and workshop of Mr Fletcher, a wheelwright. Today, the house is privately owned and not open to the public. But, it is said that, on the anniversary of his death, the priest's ghost now appears. He manifests as a shimmering, grey image, flitting about the house when the clock strikes midnight. Sometimes door latches rattle and floorboards pop to portend his appearance and, occasionally, the sound of horses galloping up to the front door accompanies the materialisation.

Tue Brook House, where the priest was petrified to death. (Discover Liverpool library)

19

THE CAVERN CLUB: WHERE MERSEYBEAT WAS BORN

Naturally, there are many places throughout Liverpool that have associations with The Beatles, and none more so than what has been named the Cavern Quarter of the city centre. Here can be found many specialist shops and bars, each one dedicated to the memory of the Fab Four. Nevertheless, the most significant of these is undoubtedly the Cavern Club.

Arguably becoming the most famous beat club in the world, the Cavern Club was originally the cellar of an early Victorian warehouse, standing at No. 10 Mathew Street. First opened as a jazz club on 16 January 1957, it was then the haunt of 'Beatniks' and 'Bohemians'. By 1960, country and western music was being performed here alongside the jazz sessions – there were no discos or DJs in those days.

Around this time too, the skiffle craze was in full swing, following the example of Lonnie Donegan (1931–2002). This gave birth to the boom in amateur and semi-professional skiffle groups all over Merseyside. One of these was The Quarrymen, of which John Lennon (1940–80) was the founder, and they first played at the Cavern in August 1957.

Soon, skiffle transposed into rhythm and blues, and then into beat music and early British rock 'n' roll. The Quarrymen transposed too, into the Silver Beatles, and then into The Beatles. It was on 17 February 1961 that The Beatles first performed at the Cavern, with Pete Best (b.1941) as drummer and with Paul McCartney (b.1942) and George Harrison (1943–2001) completing the beat combo. The Cavern then became the breeding ground for many groups and solo performers throughout the 1960s, and The Beatles went on to

Mathew Street and the Cavern Quarter. (Discover Liverpool library)

international stardom after playing the last of 275 performances there in just two years, on 3 August 1963.

The original Cavern closed in 1973, and the cellar club was filled in, in 1981, when the warehouse above it was demolished. There was a subsequent incarnation of the Cavern, just across Mathew Street, but the current Cavern Club was rebuilt on its original site in 1984.

In fact, the Liverpool architect David Backhouse was responsible for the reclamation. During this, he discovered a brick wall of arches from the rear wall of the old club, which had all the band's names still painted on it. David saved these bricks, and the wall, and now 85 per cent of the reconstructed club is built on the original basement site – and 15,000 of the bricks he used are the originals too.

One of the best features of the modern Cavern is the accurate reconstruction of the stage on which The Beatles and so many other famous performers appeared throughout three decades. It was on this stage that the Cavern Club set the feet of many local young people on the road to a career in pop music, and gave birth to the 'Mersey Sound' and to a cultural phenomenon.

During the summer of 1963, at the age of 12, I had become fascinated by the furore that The Beatles were causing in the city and was curious about the Cavern Club. So, on a Saturday morning I made a solitary trip into town and, at around ten o'clock in the morning, I made my way down to Mathew Street. This was not the tourist centre that it is today; then it was simply a narrow street of tall, shabby, decaying warehouses, many of them still functioning as such and some of them derelict.

I found the doorway to the Cavern, which was fortunately standing open. The street was deserted and so, it appeared, was the club. Quietly, and somewhat nervously, I made my way through the entrance and began to walk down a curving flight of narrow, stone steps, into the basement of the building. The daylight soon gave way to dim lights coming up from below me. I could hear no sounds of people moving about so I continued my descent.

I put my hands out against the walls to steady myself as I negotiated the steep steps, and immediately became aware of two things. One was the damp and sticky slickness of the walls, and the other, an all-pervading and increasingly overpowering smell of beer, cigarette

The Beatles playing on stage at the original Cavern Club. (Discover Liverpool library)

smoke, a general staleness, and ammonia. The wetness was residual sweat from the dancers and drinkers who had filled the Cavern the previous night, which was still sliding down the walls. The smell was the other residue of these people's presence and of their bodies!

Fighting my rising unease and slight disgust, I continued down to the club itself. There, I was surprised at how small it was, how long and narrow. The chairs and tables had all seen better days but, at the end of the low, barrel-roofed room, there was the stage with its patterned and graffitied rear wall. There was still no one around, but after a brief look around and before someone did come to chase me out, I retraced my steps and made my way back out of the dingy basement building. This time though, I kept my hands off the walls as I climbed the steps, thinking to myself, 'Well, I don't see what all the fuss is about'.

I was soon to find out, though, as was the rest of the world. In fact, I went on to be the lead singer of two rock groups in the 1960s – neither of which anyone will ever have heard of, so I won't bother repeating their names.

Today, the modern, completely reconstructed Cavern Club, and the whole Cavern Quarter, is a Mecca for tourists from all over the world. Every day, hundreds of them, in singles, couples, and groups of all sizes, cultures, and languages, can be seen taking dozens of photos. They are all capturing for themselves just a part of this very special place in the history of twentieth-century popular music and culture. Today's Cavern Club has all the atmosphere of the original venue and I heartily recommend that you experience this for yourself.

20

EVERTON AND
WAVERTREE LOCK-UPS

Crime and punishment was mainly a local affair in the centuries before the Industrial Revolution. Most villages, townships, and larger communities had their own places to lock up drunks, miscreants, ne'r-do-wells, vagabonds, and thieves. The villages that surrounded the small town of Liverpool were no exception. As localised crimes were generally petty, the places of incarceration were largely temporary and small. However, sometimes they were built to reflect a sudden rise in the level or seriousness of wrongdoing, and such was the case in the villages of Everton and Wavertree.

Towards the end of the eighteenth century, so many tourists were coming to what was then the isolated, hilltop village of Everton that it was creating a problem for the locals. The place had become famous for a number of reasons, and people were coming in increasing numbers to climb the hill to take in the fresh air and the grand views. From here, they could see the vast surrounding lands and the river and overlook the town of Liverpool, sitting at the bottom of the hill.

They also came to visit (and pull souvenir chunks out of) a historic local cottage. This had been occupied by Prince Rupert of the Rhine (1619–82) during the English Civil Wars, as he bombarded, besieged, attacked, and then largely burnt Liverpool to the ground. Because of the amount of stone being taken from the small building, it was so weakened that it ultimately had to be pulled down. So, such vandalism is nothing new!

People also came to buy Molly Bushell's famous Everton Toffee, from her village toffee shop. Everton was famous for its delicious meat pies, but tourists were also arriving to drink in the numerous taverns. However, so many rowdy young men were then getting drunk, attracting the wrong sort of young women and causing a public nuisance, that something had to be done.

So, in 1787, the villagers built a small, round, single-storey brick prison. This was known locally as 'the lockup', 'the stone jug' or, for no logical reason, 'Prince Rupert's Tower'. Mostly, it was used to incarcerate drunkards overnight, so that they might sober up.

The Everton lock-up is now the only structure left from the original village, and it still stands in the middle of what is left of the old village green. It is such a landmark that it was adopted as the central image in the emblem of Everton Football Club!

Around this time, similar problems were being experienced by the villagers of Wavertree, at the other end of the town. They had broad, open stretches of meadow and a large lake in which people would play and swim. Also, like Everton, they had many taverns offering fine ales served by hearty, buxom young women of very welcoming dispositions.

On what remains of the village green still stands today the gaol that the people of Wavertree built, in 1796, following Everton's example.

The Everton lock-up or 'the stone jug'. (Discover Liverpool library)

However, the level of law-breaking was obviously higher in Wavertree, as their lock-up had two levels! The villagers also employed a local sheriff and kitted him out with a truncheon and handcuffs. His job was to patrol the local taverns with a large handcart. With this he collected all the drunks who had been ejected by the tavern landlords and locked them up in the gaol overnight. He was paid for each man he arrested.

The Wavertree lock-up.
(Discover Liverpool library)

In the night, while the sheriff and the villagers were asleep, friends of the drunkards would climb up onto the flat, straw and lath roof, break holes in it and lower ladders and ropes so their friends could escape. They would all then return to their drinking in the morning. But, as he was paid only for each arrest, this suited the sheriff well. Also, as he was paid to make necessary repairs to the gaol, he was on a nice, regular little earner.

Towards the end of the nineteenth century, local resident and architect Sir James Picton (previously mentioned), added a pointed, slate roof and a weathervane to the lock-up, but only for aesthetic not security reasons.

Both the Everton and Wavertree lock-ups are now the only such buildings surviving in Liverpool and are Grade-II listed. They are historic and architectural treasures, despite their original purpose!

21

THE MONSTER AND THE GHOST SHIP

Both of these stories must certainly be true, as they have been told to me by many local matelots, sailors, and sons-of-the-sea, especially after I have plied them copiously with fine ales and spirits!

First, did you know that we have our own version of the Loch Ness monster? However, ours is known as the Morgawr, which is Cornish for sea monster. This bizarre sea creature actually comes from off the coast of Cornwall but, from time to time, it seems to swim northwards to cruise the waters of Liverpool Bay, especially around the coasts of the Wirral and the Isle of Man.

Many seafarers today will tell tales of this long-necked monster with its great head, beady, evil eyes, wide gash of a mouth, and rows of sharp teeth. They will also describe its massive, humped black body, covered all over with pale green patches. They will make a particular point of the fact that the beast is over 150ft (45m) long! Even so, there have been no reports of the Morgawr attacking vessels, but it can strike aggressive and threatening postures if ships sail too close to it, and it can appear and vanish with amazing speed and suddenness.

Some Liverpool mariners will also tell tales of the mysterious ghostship, the SS *President*. For well over 150 years there have been sightings, again in Liverpool Bay, of this rigged and masted paddle steamer, which, when she was commissioned in 1840, was the largest ship in the world. Setting sail from Liverpool in 1841, the luxurious vessel was bound for New York, but she never arrived – she disappeared without trace and with 136 souls on board.

For months, a watch at sea was kept for the ship, and its loss caused such a sensation that even Queen Victoria asked to be kept informed. Now, at unpredictable times, the *President* appears in our waters, suddenly coming into sight from the midst of a mysteriously materialising fog bank. Then she will disappear again into the swirling mists, just as unpredictably and just as eerily.

These are only two of the nautical tales and legends that any Liverpool sailor will be happy to tell you, especially if you too keep them liberally lubricated.

22

EDWARD RUSHTON AND THE ROYAL SCHOOL FOR THE BLIND

Across the centuries Liverpool has been blessed by so many men and women who put others before themselves, often at great personal sacrifice. I mention just two in this book and this is the first – Edward Rushton (1656–1814).

On Church Road North in Wavertree stands the Royal School for the Blind. It was originally built in 1898 to replace an older school that stood on the corner of Hardman Street and Hope Street, in the centre of Liverpool. This city school had been built in 1851, and had itself replaced the first Blind School, which had, from 1791, stood in Commutation Row, adjacent to Lime Street. It was the first such school in Britain, and had been founded by Edward Rushton. He was a Liverpool sailor and an indefatigable eighteenth-century campaigner for human rights.

Growing up in Liverpool, from the age of 11 Edward was apprenticed to a shipping company as a seaman. Indeed, he quickly became an experienced sailor and, at the age of just 16, he took the helm of a vessel in a violent storm, when the captain and crew were about to abandon ship. Edward then piloted her safely home to Liverpool. Because of this, he was promoted from his apprenticeship to the position of second mate.

In 1773, aged 17, he was serving aboard a Liverpool slave ship sailing from the Ivory Coast to Jamaica. However, there was a violent storm and the ship was wrecked. The crew, and those slaves that were not

Edward Rushton, the founder of Britain's first school
for the blind. (Discover Liverpool library)

shackled below deck, were flung into the water. Swimming towards
the safety of a floating cask, Edward discovered that a slave, named
Quamina, was already clinging to it.

Edward had already formed a close relationship with Quamina on
board ship, even though he was a slave, and he had taught the young
man to read. Seeing Edward swimming towards him, Quamina
selflessly pushed the cask towards his friend so he would be saved.
Then, bidding Edward goodbye, the slave sank to his death. This
incredible sacrifice deeply marked Rushton for the rest of his life.

The following year, when he was aged 19, Edward sailed as mate on
an American ship, which picked up slaves in Africa. It was now that

he began to recognise that human bondage and forced servitude were wrong, and this was not what he wanted to do with his life. Innately, he knew that he was obliged, as a human, to do what he could to alleviate the suffering of his enslaved fellow men and women.

Edward protested to his captain about the treatment of the captives and was threatened with being clapped in irons. Later, the slaves contracted contagious ophthalmia. This was a disease that, in most cases, brought blindness in around three weeks. The crew battened down the hatches and left the slaves without food, water, or any treatment or care whatsoever. Rushton, after more arguments with the captain, was finally allowed to take food and drink to the slaves. As a result, he caught the disease. He was himself blinded in his left eye and developed a cataract-like condition in his right eye.

Unable to continue at sea because of his blindness, Rushton returned to Liverpool and moved in with his sister. He hired local boys to read newspapers and radical literature to him every week, and he developed his political awareness as a result. Edward soon began writing poems, articles, and letters about pressing social issues of the day, especially the need to abolish slavery. He also became a tireless campaigner against the press gangs that were kidnapping sailors for forced service in the British Royal Navy.

He was also a revolutionary republican, a supporter of the French Revolution and the American War for Independence. In 1797, Edward even wrote letters to his American heroes, George Washington (1732–99) and Thomas Paine (1737–1809), the radical political theorist. He asked both men, and Washington in particular, as the former first President of America, why they were not using their public influence to oppose slavery (Washington was himself a slave owner), but neither man bothered to reply.

He next started a radical newspaper and was threatened by naval officers after he wrote articles condemning the press gangs. He also became a successful bookseller in Liverpool and, in 1784, he married Isabelle Rain. The couple went on to have five children. Eventually, he was making enough money from his bookshop to be able to afford to live comfortably and provide well for his family.

Edward was not alone in his social and political campaigns in Liverpool. With support from radical philanthropists including

William Roscoe (1753–1831), Dr James Currie (1756–1805), and William Rathbone IV (1757-1809), he established his, and Britain's, first Blind School. Admission was open only to blind residents of Lancashire and Cheshire who were between 14 and 50 years of age. They were taught handicrafts and skills by trained teachers, learning crafts including 'the winding of cotton, the spinning of worsted, the knitting of worsted stockings, the making of whip-lashes, the winding of worsted into balls and hanks for the hosiers, the picking of oakum, the making of cabbage nets, net caps, etc., the lining of hats, and music'.

In 1807, Rushton had an operation that allowed him to regain his sight. For the first time in thirty-three years, he was able to see his wife and children. Edward Rushton died of paralysis in Liverpool, on 22 November 1814.

The Blind School building on Hope Street still stands, although it is now a restaurant and offices. However, by 1893, a better-equipped and larger building had been needed and so the site in Wavertree was chosen. Throughout the years, this school has grown and been altered to keep pace with modern requirements. It is now one of the most modern facilities of its kind in Europe. The school continues to pioneer the best-quality education and services for blind and partially sighted children. The school was awarded the 'Royal' prefix by the late Queen Elizabeth II' in 1966, in recognition of its tremendous contribution.

Its continued existence is a direct tribute to, and acknowledgement of the pioneering work, determination, and strength of heart of Edward Rushton.

23

THE BLACK ROCK MERMAID OF WALLASEY

The rock on which Fort Perch Rock and the lighthouse stand, at New Brighton on Wirral, is the Black Rock. This appears on maps dating from as early as 1610. It only became known as Perch Rock from the landmark that was erected there in the nineteenth century, which was shaped like a bird's perch. But, the Black Rock it always was, and black was its reputation – not just because it was a treacherous hazard to sailing ships, but because of the mermaid.

In the eighteenth century, and into the nineteenth century too, tales were told of the bewitching creature, with the naked torso of a dazzlingly beautiful maiden and the lower body of a fish, but with scales that glistened in a myriad of ever-changing colours. These seemed to hypnotise sailors as they sailed by her in their boats. But it was her womanly charms that really captured their rapt attention, as she sat on the Black Rock, gazing out to sea and slowly combing her long, thick, shiningly flaxen tresses, in the full bloom of youthful womanhood. Then, she would begin to sing a song in a strange language, and with an eerie melody that nevertheless pierced hearts and souls with a combination of melancholy and ecstasy, leaving the listener spellbound and unable to resist her call. Even the most hardened and experienced old salt, well versed in the ways of the deep and the wily sea creatures that dwelt beneath its waves, would be ensnared and drawn towards the Black Rock mermaid.

As was young John Robinson.

A story tells how, in the late 1700s, this young mariner had been shipwrecked off the north Wales coast, but had managed to haul himself, the only survivor, into the stricken ship's little jolly boat, which had also survived the wreck. The tale then tells how he was 'tossed on the ocean for six days and nights' before reaching the stormy waters off the Black Rock at Wallasey. Here, to his amazement, he heard the siren song of the watery, winsome enchantress.

He steered his tiny craft closer inland, unable to resist and heedless of the dangers from the deadly rocks and shoals. Then he saw her, in all her beauteous, wanton glory and scintillating many-hued colours. 'Come aboard, fair maiden of the sea!' he called to her, now completely enraptured.

And she immediately did as she was bidden. Laying her golden comb on the rock, she dived into the sea and swam with incredible speed to John's boat. Next, in one smooth, agile sweep, she leapt out of the water and sat beside John in the small vessel. The young sailor could not take his amazed gaze from the sea maiden's charms. His heart raced faster and faster, and his pulse began to surge so much his head swam.

The tale then tells how John forced himself to resist the temptations that were now overwhelming him, and he and the maid simply talked for a long while. Then, without warning, the mermaid fell into John's arms and kissed him like he had never been kissed before in his young seafaring life. She almost drew his breath entirely from his body. Next, and just as abruptly, she leapt overboard and dived under the waves, but not before giving the breathless, hapless youth her ring as a keepsake.

John called for her. Searched for her. Rowed as close to the Black Rock as he dared, but he saw no sign of the sea siren, nor did he hear her song any more.

John Robinson made it safely to Liverpool, where he was greeted by his friends, who had heard of the shipwreck and were amazed at his survival. They were even more amazed when he told them the tale of his encounter with the Black Rock mermaid. At first, his friends did not believe him, until he proved the truth of his tale by showing them the fish maiden's ring. It was wrought in a complex and intricate weaving of gold and silver strands, and with a strange device engraved on its surface, which seemed to be of a sea serpent.

'For that is what she truly was,' said one of John's older sailor friends. 'I know of this treacherous maid. She is indeed a serpent of the deep, who transforms herself into a comely wench to lure men to their deaths on the Black Rock. Or she toys with them, as she has done with you John.'

But the young sailor laughed this off, saying that he was in love with the maiden of the sea, and would seek her out the following day.

But this was not to be, for when he took to his bed that night his heart began to ache with an anguish of lost love that left him hollow and bereft. It ate at him, withered his will and his strength, seemed to drain the very life out of him. And John moaned and wept for his lost love from beneath the sea and, after five days, he pined himself to death.

So, be warned! If you are ever sailing past the Black Rock and you hear the siren song of the sea maiden, and you see her sitting on the rock with her golden comb running through her golden hair, resist and sail away! Otherwise, you too will fall so helplessly in love with this fatal temptress that your life will not be worth a Spanish doubloon or a golden guinea!

The Black Rock mermaid.
(Discover Liverpool library)

24

THE THUGS OF WILLALOO

By the middle decades of the nineteenth century, in what is now the north end of South Street in Toxteth and in the area known as the 'Welsh Streets', a small community of single- and two-storey cottages had grown up. This was known as Willaloo.

Surrounded mostly by open heathland, watered by a few brooks and streams, this was quite an isolated community. Nevertheless, it was a busy one, with three very popular beer houses named after their landlords: Chadwick's, Brookfield's, and Lee's.

On the site of the present Wynnstay, Veolas, Rhiwlas, and Powis Streets, not far from modern Princes Road and Princes Park Gates, stood a large tannery yard. Workers from here packed into these watering holes. So, too, did the workers from the nearby Dingle Iron Foundry in Horsfall Street, known as the Mersey Forge (and previously described), as well as employees from a large ships' carpenter's works on the riverfront. The local residents also regularly frequented these out-of-the-way drinking dens, especially on Sundays.

Willaloo was also very popular with sailors because of the cheap ale and even cheaper women, whose morals and fees were very flexible. This was a place were virtually 'anything went'. Deals were done, contraband was bought and sold, and drunkenness was the general condition. This became a notorious community, well known around Liverpool town as the hub of nefarious doings, dastardly deeds, and for disturbance and disorder.

It was a rough, tough, and uncompromising neighbourhood, where at least two or three bouts of bare-knuckle boxing would take place every Sunday evening, just before dinnertime. These attracted large crowds of spectators, fuelled gambling, and led to frequent and vicious fights among the crowds: Everyone was working up an appetite for their hearty evening meal. In fact, anyone who just wanted a good fight, for fun if not for profit, would start in on any likely candidates standing around! These outbreaks of unbridled aggression often grew into a bloody mêlée of writhing, bruised, and broken male bodies, although dozens of women often threw themselves into the mix, too, fighting between themselves as well as in amongst the men!

Many an old score was settled in the beer houses and streets of Willaloo, and many new feuds began here too. This became such a tradition, especially in the 1830s, that official lookouts were posted to keep 'cavey' for the 'Rozzers'.

But there were only two police constables in the district, whose names were Officers Lunt and Lowey. These men were based in the Toxteth Bridewell in Cotter Street, which was over half a mile away (and no longer exists). This meant that the fights were only very rarely officially broken up. The beer houses became notorious and Willaloo infamous as a district that was not for the faint-hearted, nor for those of a nervous or sensitive disposition!

Chadwick's and Brookfield's beer houses had closed before 1870, but Lee's survived well into the 1920s, as this was on the fringe of the neighbourhood. However, Willaloo has long gone. It was completely

Despite appearances to the contrary, this was the violent community of Willaloo. (Liverpool Athenaeum library)

demolished and the site cleared in the 1870s. It was replaced by ranks of Victorian houses that transformed the open heathland of old Toxteth into the working-class hinterland of modern 'Liverpool 8'. These homes were constructed by firms of Welsh builders, who gave the Welsh names to the streets that they laid out.

Willaloo is now largely forgotten, and today the only thing that this area of Toxteth is famous for is No. 9 Madryn Street, which was the first childhood home of Ringo Starr (b.1940).

25

'AND DID THOSE FEET ...?': BIDSTON HALL AND THE HOLY GRAIL

One of the many legends associated with ancient and mysterious Bidston Hill and its medieval hall, on the Wirral Peninsula, tells that Saint Joseph of Arimathea visited the hill in ancient times. He was a wealthy merchant and the uncle of the Virgin Mary, and so the great-uncle of Jesus. Joseph sailed the known world, trading in a range of commodities, and is said to have visited England to buy Cornish tin. He also brought Jesus with him to England when the future messiah was still a young boy.

The English poet William Blake (1757–1827) used this legend when he was writing the poem that we now know as 'Jerusalem'. In it, he asks if Jesus did indeed come to England:

And did those feet, in ancient times, walk upon England's mountains green?
And was the Holy Lamb of God, in England's pleasant pastures seen?
And did the countenance divine, shine forth upon our crowded hills?
And was Jerusalem builded here, amongst those dark satanic mills?

Joseph is also said to have donated the tomb in which Christ's body was laid after the crucifixion and before the resurrection. After this, it is said that the saint returned to Britain to bring Christianity to the pagan natives. He had been sent here, with other disciples, by St Philip. He brought two vials with him to England this time. One of these contained the blood of Jesus and the other contained his sweat. Both were taken by Joseph from Christ as he hung on the cross.

Local legends tell of Joseph of Arimathea visiting many places in England, as well as Bidston Hill. He is also said to have brought the Holy Grail with him to England. This was the chalice that Jesus and his disciples used at the Last Supper, on the eve of Good Friday.

The most well-known story says that Joseph of Arimathea hid the Grail in a well at Glastonbury, now called the Chalice Well, but it has never been found there. This may well be because, as another legend tells, he actually hid it in a cave under the site of a hunting lodge that would eventually become the present Bidston Hall!

Of the many tales associated with King Arthur, the Knights of the Round Table, and their search for the Holy Grail, there is one that comes from an ancient and famous fourteenth-century poem, 'Sir Gawain and the Green Knight'. In the story, the noble Sir Gawain searches all over the Wirral for the Grail, including at the Green Chapel, accompanied by Sir John Stanley from Bidston Hall. Here,

Bidston Hall. Was this the Green Chapel of the Green Knight? (Discover Liverpool library)

he faces a challenge to mortal combat from the fearsome Green Knight.

Sir Gawain's opponent is completely green, from his clothes and hair to his beard and skin, except for his eyes, which burn with red flame. Ultimately victorious, loyal and pure Sir Gawain searches in and around the Green Chapel for the Grail. Did he find it? What happened to Sir Gawain? I suggest that you read the poem.

Some people believe that the original Bidston Hall was, in fact, the legendary Green Chapel from the poem. Could this mean, therefore, that the lost Holy Grail might still be waiting to be discovered at Bidston?

26

LEASOWE CASTLE AND THE DERBY RACES

Leasowe Castle on Wirral stands on the shore between Leasowe Lighthouse and Leasowe Golf Club. It is an attractive, if odd agglomeration of construction from many centuries, and in a number of architectural styles.

The main feature of the old structure is its octagonal, crenelated central tower. This was the original castle and was erected in 1593 by Ferdinando Stanley (b.1559), 5th Earl of Derby. The following year, he was awarded the manor of Wallasey and became the Mayor of Liverpool.

However, the earl upset some Catholics when he refused to accept their offer to depose Queen Elizabeth I and claim the throne for himself. Ferdinando suddenly took severely ill with drastic vomiting. Quite soon afterwards, he died on 16 April 1594, in unexplained circumstances. Poisoning by disgruntled Jesuits was suspected, and he had apparently asked his doctors to stop treating him as he knew he was dying. Ferdinando's stablemaster was accused of conspiracy to murder his master and, unsurprisingly, galloped away on one of the earl's best horses. The man was never seen again.

When Ferdinando had built his castle at Leasowe, he named it 'New Hall' and used it mainly as a hunting lodge. He had constructed it to be particularly tall, with a broad, flat roof to use as an observation tower. From this, he and his friends could watch his regular horse races along the Leasowe shoreline. The tower's entrance door was set about 6ft (1.8m) above ground level, to protect it from the high tides that are still common on that coastal area.

Ferdinando's brother, William Stanley (1561–1642), inherited the earldom as the 6th Earl of Derby. He was as passionate about horse racing as Ferdinando and, sometime between 1600 and 1642, William added a large stable block and four square towers to the castle. The land around the castle was open and flat, so it was ideal for horse races, and the Earls of Derby were lavish hosts to their guests. Indeed, they attracted many illustrious individuals to watch the races, to enter their own horses, and on occasion to take to the racing saddle themselves.

However, even though these were races organised by the Derbys, they were never the official Derby Horse Race. This was first run at Newmarket and was the idea of Edward Smith-Stanley (1752–1834), the 12th Earl of Derby. That story is told in *More Merseyside Tales*.

In the autumn of 1682, the race meeting held at Leasowe had a very prominent visitor and jockey, in the person of James Scott (1649–85), the 1st Duke of Monmouth. He was the illegitimate son of King Charles II (1630–85), and he attended the meeting with a great crowd of friends. He was joined there by the Mayor of Chester with a troop of forty horsemen. There was also a large crowd of people from Chester, as well as locals, who had arrived to see the duke as much as the races.

The first competition, with a prize of £60 (£10,000 today), was won by Monmouth riding his own horse. Although it was whispered that he had been allowed to win, nobody raised any objections!

Ever the sportsman, Monmouth also agreed to race on foot, twice, with a Mr Cutts of Cambridge. The first race he ran stripped naked and the second in just his boots. The duke won both times, to the delight of the crowds – for many reasons!

When the people back in Chester received the news about the duke's stunning victories, the city was delighted. Fireworks were set off and people danced around bonfires as church bells rang. The duke and his party had been invited to the city to join in the celebrations. When they arrived they were feted, sumptuously fed and watered, and entertained lavishly in the mayor's house.

Unfortunately, on the death of his father, Monmouth tried to claim the throne for himself and was found guilty of treason. He was executed on Tower Hill by the notoriously incompetent Jack Ketch (d.1686), who took around eight or nine strokes of the axe. Even then, the duke's head had to be finally severed using a knife.

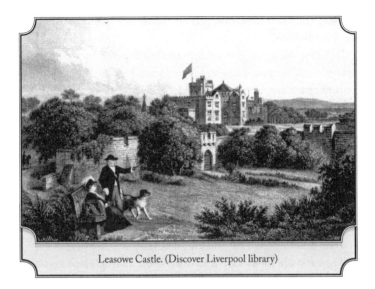
Leasowe Castle. (Discover Liverpool library)

During the English Civil Wars, from 1642 to 1651, when Royalist aristocrats had their houses and estates confiscated by Parliament, Leasowe Castle passed into the hands of Cromwellian supporters. It was neglected and became very dilapidated. The Leasowe horse races continued though, under the auspices of a variety of aristocrats and local landowners. They were always popular and well attended by crowds of spectators. The location of the main racecourse now lies under what is now Leasowe Golf Course.

With the restoration of the monarchy in 1660, most Royalists had their property returned to them, including the Earls of Derby. By the late eighteenth century, though, they had given up all interest in Leasowe Castle. So much so that it was eventually named 'Mockbeggar Hall' by locals and travellers. This was because calling there in the hope of receiving food or shelter would have been futile. It was from this time, too, that one of the most dangerous sandbanks off the north Wallasey coast was named 'Mockbeggar Bank'.

Leasowe Castle changed ownership several times over the years, although it was used as a family residence throughout most of its life. From 1821 to 1895, it was owned by the Cust family and the entrance gateway carries their family crest. Their motto is carved on the lintel, reading, '*Qui Cust Odit Caveat*'. This translates as 'He Who Cust Hates Let Him Beware!'

In 1896, the castle was sold at auction for sum of £7,000, and opened as the licensed Leasowe Castle Hotel. Then, in 1910, it became a convalescent and retirement home for railway workers until 1970.

The old building now became derelict once more, until 1982, when it was rescued, restored, and renovated by an enthusiastic local businessman. He reopened it once more as a hotel. In recent years, it has been fully modernised again, with the addition of a health centre and spa.

Leasowe Castle Hotel combines ancient and modern in its architecture and setting and is a real asset to redeveloping tourist offer in North Wirral. However, Leasowe Castle has a number of ghosts, and one haunting has a particularly grisly story attached to it.

At one stage in its varied history, the building came into the possession of a man who was involved in a bitter feud with some of his neighbours. This belligerent landowner captured among his prisoners a father and son, whom he locked up in the old pile. They were incarcerated in a room that is still panelled in oak originally taken from the submerged prehistoric forest that lies off the nearby Meols shore.

In a frenzy of fear, the imprisoned father killed his son and then committed suicide by battering out his own brains against the wall. Many years later, when the castle was first converted into a hotel, guests frequently reported seeing ghosts of an older and younger man standing by their bedsides. Guests also occasionally complained about their blood being chilled by dreadful screams issuing from what is now named the Oak Room. Occasionally, these ghosts can still be seen today, although thankfully the screaming has stopped!

27

WAVERTREE GARDEN SUBURB

So many social, environmental, and community innovations have been pioneered on Merseyside and, just outside the heart of the Liverpool suburb of Wavertree village, is the picturesque urban haven that is Wavertree Garden Suburb.

It grew from the 'Garden Cities' movement in the early years of the twentieth century. This was a period when enlightened and philanthropic entrepreneurs and architects were trying to combine modernity with a 'rural idyll'. Their aim was to construct attractively built, artistically designed, yet fully equipped houses and cottages to meet the needs of an expanding, modern, urban, mixed community. They wanted this to be set in surroundings that they felt represented the best of country life. This would mean lots of green space, trees, and shrubs, in an open-garden setting with a wide range of appropriate community amenities. This kind of civic town planning had been inspired by communities established by philanthropic, nineteenth-century entrepreneurs, such as the Cadburys at Bournville; Titus Salt in Saltaire, Yorkshire; William Hartley, with Hartley's Village at Aintree; and Lord Leverhulme at Port Sunlight on the Wirral.

The land was obtained at advantageous terms on a 999-year lease from its owner, the Marquis of Salisbury, who was the lord of the manor of much of Liverpool's southern and eastern suburbs (the current marquis still owns the manors of many Liverpool suburbs). Wavertree Garden Suburb was to be one of about twenty or so similar developments planned to be built up and down the country in the decade before the First World War. And so, in 1910, the small community of Wavertree Nook became the site of one of England's first garden suburbs. Additional houses and gardens were to be built between Thingwall Road and Queens Drive over the following five years.

The project was a co-partnership housing scheme, which meant that the houses were owned neither individually nor by a profit-seeking private landlord. The owner of the whole estate was a company called Liverpool Garden Suburb Tenants Ltd, in which the tenants of the houses were themselves shareholders. Outsiders could also purchase shares, and the annual dividend was generally limited to around 5 per cent.

The suburb was created around existing roads, with Heywood Road, Wavertree Nook Road, and Thingwall Road providing a frame for the new 'urban village'. The first phase covered 25 acres with just eleven houses per acre. This gives a clear indication of the spaciousness of the overall concept. The houses were built in a Victorian, mock-Tudor style, with variations on this common theme.

Emphasis was given to open space and to juxtaposing detached, semi-detached, and terraced properties. In Fieldway, a circle of these mixed properties was constructed around a large central green and, in an adjacent part of the suburb, a bowling green and tennis courts were provided. There was also a children's playground with swings, slides, maypoles, and roundabouts, as well as football pitches. Trees were planted throughout, and especially on the margins of the wide pavements. These included beeches, elms, sycamores, birches and, to the delight of local boys particularly, horse chestnuts (conkers)!

The grand opening took the form of a large garden fete on the green, with music, Morris dancers and tableaux, and with tea, cakes, and minerals. This was such a popular success that, before long, open-air parliaments, maypole dancing, rose queen pageants, public lectures, arts and crafts, and other educational classes were taking place on the green.

A Community Institute was built on Thingwall Road, to accommodate the meetings of clubs and societies, celebrations, amateur dramatics, and concerts. There was also a purpose-built row of shops in Wavertree Nook, specially designed to meet every household need, from butcher to baker to candlestick maker (well almost). Many of these local amenities still exist.

This original garden suburb area was going to be just the start of a much larger estate, and the suburb was intended to spread at least across the other side of Queens Drive towards Childwall. All was going well until the First World War broke out in 1914. All plans now had to be put on hold.

After the war there were new priorities because money and manpower were now in short supply. This meant that the garden suburb did not expand beyond its current borders, nor did the movement begin to take root in other parts of Liverpool, as had been hoped. Indeed, when construction ceased in 1915, only 360 houses had been built out of a planned 1,800. In the 1930s, Liverpool Garden Suburb Tenants Ltd began to sell off its houses to individual owner-occupiers and, by 1938, the company had been liquidated.

And yet, the fact that the original plans for a much larger community were not realised is what makes the suburb so unique. It has an eccentric charm, but most of all it continues unspoilt, into the twenty-first century. The neighbourhood is an island of enlightened aspiration in a sea of otherwise mundane suburbia. Fortunately, Liverpool City Council declared the suburb a conservation area in 1971, guaranteeing its unspoilt survival.

Wavertree Garden Suburb will always have a special place in my heart because I played there as a child, especially in the playground, had friends there, went to school near there (both primary and

Wavertree Garden Suburb today – Fieldway, the entrance to The Green. (Discover Liverpool library)

secondary), and we did our family shopping in the shops at Wavertree Nook. As a young boy, I saw my first amateur dramatic performance in the Wavertree Garden Suburb Institute, and as an 11 and 12-year-old boy I earned extra money by cutting hedges and doing the gardening for householders throughout the suburb. I charged 4 shillings an hour, which was a high rate sixty years ago. Even so, I did provide quality work, had a long list of regular clients, and lots of repeat work! This was also a very lucrative area to raise money when I was a cub and a boy scout, during Bob-a-Job Week. If I ever want to bask in nostalgia and very happy memories, a slow stroll around tranquil Wavertree Garden Suburb will do the trick.

28

THE PYRAMID TOMB
OF RODNEY STREET

Rodney Street is one of the broad thoroughfares that run through the Georgian quarter of Liverpool, just to the east of the city centre. In the graveyard of the former Church of Saint Andrew lies the body of one of the city's most prominent Victorians, in a tomb beneath a pyramid.

His name was William McKenzie, and he was born in Scotland in 1794. William came to Liverpool to follow his career as a civil engineer, building canals and railways in the burgeoning town. He was a great success and a pioneer in his field. He also won the respect of his peers and the admiration of the public. He died in 1851 and, as he had no children, he passed the bulk of his £340,000 estate to his brother in his will – the equivalent of £36,770,000 today!.

However, the fact that he died with such conspicuous wealth gave rise to much gossip. How did he amass such a fortune? Why is his tomb such a peculiar shape? Over time, a legend grew to answer both of these questions and, in the last 150 years, this tale has become an established part of Liverpool folklore.

The story says that William McKenzie was an avid and unusually successful poker player. To guarantee his success at cards, the whispered story went, William had sold his soul to the Devil. This was to be claimed by 'Old Nick', according to the terms of a blood-signed pact, once William was 'buried beneath the ground'.

So, in an attempt to thwart the Devil, McKenzie reasoned that if his body was not buried under the ground then the Devil could not claim his soul. This was why, the tale tells, in his will he also stipulated that he should be entombed above ground. He is said to be seated upright at a card table, holding a winning hand of cards and so 'cocking a snook' at

The pyramid tomb of William McKenzie. (Discover Liverpool library)

the Devil. In theory, because William had thwarted the precise wording of the pact, the Lord of Hell could not claim his prize of the canny Scotsman's soul.

Those who believe this story – and a surprising number of people do – say that he sits there still, inside the pyramid-shaped tomb in the centre of the graveyard. However, a ghostly figure wearing a frock coat and top hat is frequently sighted around Rodney Street and its side streets and alleys. People say that this is the restless spectre of William McKenzie, denied eternal rest in Heaven because of his devilish pact. So perhaps the Devil is extracting his due after all!

Despite the enduring popularity of this story, it is important to point out that the curiously shaped tomb itself was, in fact, erected seventeen years after McKenzie's death. The inscription on the door of the pyramid itself explains:

In the vault beneath lie the remains of William MacKenzie of Newbie Dumfriesshire, Esquire,
who died 29th October 1851 aged 57 years.

Also, Mary his wife, who died 19th December 1838, aged 48 years,
and Sarah, his second wife who died 9th December 1867, aged 60 years.
This monument was erected by his Brother Edward as a token of love
and affection A.D. 1868.
The memory of the just is blessed.

So, this rather makes the story of McKenzie himself building the
pyramid to thwart the Devil a bit redundant. But, as is so often the
case, some people never let the truth get in the way of a good yarn!

St Andrew's Church itself was built in 1824 to serve the large
community of ex-patriate Scots, of which William McKenzie and his
brother were members. It closed through lack of use in 1975, and was
left derelict for decades following an arson attack in 1983.

The building was rescued by Liverpool City Council in 2008,
and the decay was halted. It has now been completely restored and
refurbished, and has been converted into a very attractive complex
of student apartments, while retaining all of the original external
architectural features.

William McKenzie's pyramid-shaped tomb makes a very unusual
ornament to the building, sitting in the centre of the graveyard
next door. At least the students don't have noisy neighbours, nor
do I imagine they get any complaints from William and the other
residents of the graveyard about any disturbance that the young
people themselves may cause!

THE NEW BRIGHTON WAXWORKS CHAMBER OF HORRORS

Liverpool may have had its waxworks in the Museum of Anatomy, but so did Wirral. This was in the basement of the New Brighton Tower Building and was an added attraction to the rides and amusements in the fairground on the resort's seafront. The most popular attraction inside the waxworks, though, was undoubtedly the Chamber of Horrors.

Just as the anatomy exhibits in Liverpool attracted a certain kind of clientele, so too did the grislier exhibits in this particular collection. According to an original guidebook, among the displays to be seen here were the following:

> The scene before us is at Gibbet Hall, Hindhead, Surrey, where the murderers of a sailor expiated their crime. The sailor was tramping from Portsmouth, upon him was a purse of gold, his leave pay, when he encountered three villains who attacked him, cut his throat and stripped the body. The corpse was discovered by a labourer who remembered seeing the sailor, and the three men who had endeavoured to sell the victim's clothes. They were arrested, tried at Kingston, and condemned to death.

Also on display was the drunkard's cloak. This was a large barrel or tub with arm holes in the sides and a hole in the top, which was dropped over the head, shoulders, and body, down to their knees:

The victim [...] was led through the town to the view of all beholders and as an example to all other drunkards. It should be noted that what is peculiar to this particular torture is that the prisoner is unable to feed himself, and the only food he or she obtained is that which was actually given by another person.

The entrance to the Tower Waxworks.
(Discover Liverpool library)

The scold's bridle, also known as a 'gossip's bridle' or the 'branks', was a kind of metal muzzle that completely enclosed the head, with a plate that pressed the tongue down inside the mouth, sometimes with spikes in it. Wives who were seen as witches, or 'shrews' and 'scolds', were forced to wear the bridle locked onto their head:

> Used for women only, the 'shrew or chiding and scolding woman'. The one shown depicts a woman who has slandered her neighbours and friends.

Liverpool's stocks and pillory, as well as the town ducking stool, which were all in regular use, were all located near to where the modern town hall stands on Dale Street:

> This scene is opposite an old country Inn, where the unlucky ones are pelted with rotten eggs. This was a common sight in almost every town and village. The Pillory is where the condemned malefactors for innumerable minor offences were fastened, in full view of the public as shown in the tableau.

The rack:

> In the scene before us Guy Fawkes is being racked – He plotted to blow up James I and his Parliament on the 5th November, 1650. Caught red-handed he was asked what the purpose was of so many barrels of gunpowder, he replied, 'To blow the Scotsmen back to Scotland'. He stubbornly refused to divulge the names of his accomplices, was tortured on the rack and eventually confessed.

Branding:

> The tableau before us shows James Nayler, a Quaker, who claimed to be the Messiah. The punishment inflicted being that of 'Branding' – being guilty of horrid blasphemy and that he was a grand impostor, his tongue should be bored through with a red-hot iron, and that he should be stigmatised on the forehead with a letter 'B'.

The sentence was carried out in December 1656, and he was then imprisoned for two years. Branding was totally abolished in England in 1879.

Pressing to death (*peine forte de dure*) was a dreadful form of execution also carried out within the walls of Liverpool Tower, during the reign of Queen Anne (1702–1707). This grim bastion stood at the bottom of Water Street, where modern Tower Building now stands:

> This barbarous torture originated in England about 1406. The last reported case, from Ireland, was in 1740. It was instituted to make a prisoner plead guilty, in which case all his property went to the Crown. The scene depicts Thomas Spiggot, a highwayman, who suffered this torture in January 1721, beneath the Old Bailey. The third figure is an official waiting for the moment when the prisoner may decide to plead.

The boots:

> Another old-time torture, the prisoner having one of his feet in a large Iron Boot filled with cold water, whilst the other in another Iron Boot in which molten metal was poured.
>
> From the expression on the prisoner's face it can be taken that it was hardly a 'party game'.

The Chamber of Horrors also featured a 'Tableau of Arthur Alfred Rouse, the murderous commercial traveller, on the Scaffold with the Chaplain, Warder, and his Executioner'. Among other notorious characters displayed were:

> William Fish (Blackburn murderer)
> David Davies (the murdering Dartmoor Shepherd)
> Samuel Herbert Dougal (the Moat Farm murderer)
> George Smith (the Brides in the Bath murderer)
> John Schneider (the Bakehouse murderer)
> John Jackson (Strangeways Prison murderer)
> Mrs. Berry (the Oldham murderess)

… and Dr. Hawley Harvey Crippen (the London Cellar Murderer) and Ethel Le Neve, his Mistress.

Crippen was brought to justice thanks to the evidence of Mary (known as 'Ma') Egerton, the Liverpool pub landlady and theatrical agent.

The waxworks had opened almost as soon as had the tower itself in 1896, and it remained popular across the decades. It was a fashionable pastime to spend a night locked in the waxworks, particularly in the 1950s and 1960s, generally to win a bet and only with the permission of the management. However, few people came out unscathed in the morning. More often than not, they emerged from the basement in the morning reporting mysterious, loud and unnerving creakings and groanings, which lasted throughout the night, These, they said, seemed to come from the walls and ceiling all around.

What people did not know – but the management did – was that every night, and after very heavy usage, the sprung floor in the ballroom directly above the waxworks made all these noises as the springs slowly retracted and the parquet flooring reset itself.

New Brighton Tower building, including the waxworks and its Chamber of Horrors, was totally destroyed in a catastrophic fire in 1969.

30

₮HE ₱EMON AND
₮HE ₿IN ₣IELD

For this next story, we return to Wavertree once more – one of Liverpool's richest locations for curious tales. In the village, the roads opposite the Bluecoat School and Holy Trinity Church, further up the hill on Church Road, was once a large area of open land. This was part of the Great Heath (or Waste) that I mentioned previously. Standing here and serving the people of Wavertree, Childwall, and other local communities was a large windmill.

People were obliged by law to bring their grain to be ground at this mill, and to others around the country. This was because all such mills were owned by the monarch by 'right of soke'. The sovereign derived income from charging for this and he or she would pay the miller's wages from it. Frequently, a soke mill was rented or leased out to a local aristocrat or landowner, who would then take a share of the income. This was the case with the mill at Wavertree, which was called the King's Mill.

First appearing in records dating from 1452, the mill remained the property of the crown until 1639, when King Charles I (1600–49) granted it to James Stanley (1607–51), who would become the 7th Earl of Derby. By 1676, the mill was in the possession of William Stanley (1656–1702), the 9th Earl of Derby.

The new owners kept the right of soke, so their tenants were still forbidden to have their corn ground anywhere else. In 1768, the ownership of the mill passed to Bamber Gascoyne (1725–91) of Childwall Hall, the ancestor of the late *University Challenge* Bamber Gascoigne (1935–2022). It was subsequently owned by the Marquesses of Salisbury and was finally leased by a Colonel James Bourne.

The old mill falling derelict in 1909. (Liverpool Athenaeum library)

As Liverpool began to grow during the eighteenth century, it needed stone for new buildings. This was soon being quarried from all around the town, including from the land upon which stood the Wavertree King's Mill. Obviously, the mill could not be touched and must be allowed to continue to operate unrestricted, so stone was quarried from the land around three sides of the mill. Eventually, the mill was left standing out into the large quarry, on a promontory of rock, with a strip of land still connecting it to the village. This was just wide enough to allow a loaded donkey or cart to make its way to and from the mill. Enough land was also left unquarried for the miller's house.

However, by the mid-nineteenth century, all was not well because the quarrying had been very deep. A local legend tells how things began to go wrong in the village.

People were falling sick and dying without any apparent cause. A boy was blown off the track to the mill by an unexpected gust of heavy wind. He died from his injuries at the bottom of the quarry. In 1866, 10-year-old Richard Matthews from the village was struck by the mill vanes and killed outright. A few years later, the long hair of the miller's daughter was caught by the rotating vanes and it was ripped out by the roots. She was injured but survived.

This all meant that – obviously – the quarrying had been so deep that a demon from hell had been awoken and he was taking revenge on the village.

The priest was consulted for a solution. He instructed that every night, when the miller had finished his day's work, he should tether the vanes of the mill in the position of a cross. The moonlight would then cast the shadow of this onto the quarry and the demon would be quieted. The miller followed these instructions and, sure enough, the catastrophes stopped and the sick recovered.

The mill ceased grinding corn in 1890, and the quarry also fell into disuse. From this time, the great hole in the ground was used as a dump for ash and waste from across Liverpool. Within a few years, it was filled in back up to the original level and became known as the 'Bin Field'.

The old mill, which people avoided as it was believed to be haunted, was damaged in a great storm in 1895. It was beyond repair and the ruin stood until 1916, when it was demolished. Between the world wars, the Bin Field was built over with the roads and houses that stand there still. The site of the Old Mill is in Beverley Road.

In 1986, prior to the building of two new houses on the site, an archaeological dig was undertaken and the foundations of the mill were excavated. The old mill stones and a commemorative plaque are displayed in the front garden of one of the houses.

31

EVERTON BEACON:
FIRES AND FLAGS

The summit of Everton Ridge, upon which the village grew, is an exceptionally historic part of Liverpool. Everton predated the city as a settlement as far back as Roman times. Because the ridge is the highest hill for miles around, it is a strategic location. This is why the Italian invaders, the Vikings, Normans, and Prince Rupert of the Rhine in 1644, wanted to take command of it.

After the founding of Liverpool by King John (1166–1216) in 1207, a tall watchtower was built here. It is mentioned in records dating from 1220. What became known as Everton Beacon was 6 yards (5.5m) square and 25ft (7.75m) high. It was constructed in plain stone and gave unobstructed views of the land for miles around, including the river, Wirral, and Wales.

The viewing platform was on the flat roof, which was surrounded by a crenelated parapet. Immediately below this was the guardroom, with a kitchen area at ground level. This was still standing in 1588, when a beacon fire was lit upon the roof, warning of the sailing of the Spanish Armada. This linked with beacon fires on other high points around the region and the country. Of course, we defeated the Spanish!

In peaceful times, the Everton Beacon was a popular gathering place for picnics on the surrounding grass, again because of the fine views of the river and surrounding countryside, and for the fresh air. Indeed, early in the reign of King Charles I (1600–40), people climbed up to the top of the beacon to get married.

At the outbreak of the Napoleonic Wars (1803–15), a lookout garrison was stationed here to light a beacon fire if necessary. This would warn of any sightings of the French fleet sailing up the Mersey.

Everton Beacon. (Liverpool Athenaeum library)

Barrels of turpentine and pitch were kept in the guardroom for the purpose. Fortunately, the enemy fleet never came and the beacon fire remained unlit.

However, by the late 1700s the ancient watchtower had become unsafe. Discussions were under way to decide whether or not to take it down when, on a very stormy night late in 1803, it blew down anyway.

But the war with France was still in full force and an early warning system was still required. So, in 1804, a mechanical semaphore signal station was built to replace the beacon. This consisted of an upright post with three extended arms on each side. There was also a system of flag poles, and the signal arms and flags could be positioned in a variety of combinations. In this way, messages could be transmitted to another signal station across the river on Wirral, at the top of Bidston Hill.

When the beacon site was being cleared and new foundations were being laid for the semaphore station, the bodies of two Roundhead soldiers were found buried. This raised lots of questions, not least being who were they? Who killed them? Why were they killed? And why were they buried here? These have never been answered.

Were they spies who had been captured and executed during the Civil War by soldiers of Prince Rupert of the Rhine? He had occupied a cottage in Everton village, at the top of the ridge, whilst he planned his siege of Liverpool in 1644. He also stationed his army on the ridge, consisting of 10,000 men, plus cavalry and cannon.

The signal station was abandoned as the French war drew to a close, and the Duke of Wellington (1769–1852) defeated Napoleon Bonaparte (1769–1821) at the Battle of Waterloo in 1815. However, the signal station had been cleared away the previous year.

In its place, the magnificent Church of St George was built, opening also in 1815. Here the beautiful church still stands, dominating the skyline overlooking Liverpool. With its vibrant congregation and important role in the community, it is known as the Iron Church and is Grade-I listed. It was the first of three churches built in cast iron and sold in self-assembly kit form comprising many component parts.

This was the innovative idea of the Warrington-born ironmaster, John Cragg (1767–1854), with his architect partner, Thomas Rickman (1776–1841). They designed and built the kits at Cragg's Mersey Iron Foundry in Tithebarn Street, in Liverpool town centre. The second of Cragg's churches also still stands. This is St Michael's, in the village of St Michael's-in-the-Hamlet, near Aigburth. The third was St Philip's in Hardman Street, but this was demolished in 1882.

The views from the top of Everton Ridge are still stunning. On a clear day, one can see right across the Wirral Peninsula to north Wales, as well as out to the windfarms in Liverpool Bay, and beyond to the Irish Sea. All this from the acres of rolling open land of Everton Park. It is quite special to stand there, looking out across the land and seascape, in the knowledge that the hill and the ancient village have played such significant roles in our remarkable history.

32

THE OWEN & WILLIAM OWEN ELIAS STREETS

During the late nineteenth century, Welsh builders came to Liverpool and constructed many of our streets of terraced houses. These are usually identifiable by their roofs, made of slate that was quarried and mined in north Wales.

One company in particular was very active, especially in the north of the city. This was the family firm of Owen & William Owen Elias. They built houses in and around Everton and Walton, between County Road and Goodison Road.

The father-and-son firm decided to immortalise themselves in the process, so they spelt out the name of their company in the initial letters of the names they gave to the streets that they created. In order, these are: **O**wen, **W**inslow, **E**ton, **N**eston, **A**ndrew, **N**imrod, **D**ane, **W**ilburn, **I**smay, **L**ind, **L**owell, **I**ndex, and **A**rnot Streets.

On the other side of County Road, the sequence carries on with: **M**akin, **O**lney, **W**eldon, **E**uston, and **N**ixon Streets.

To complete the run, the sequence is reversed on the other side of Bedford Road, with **E**lton, **L**iston, **I**mrie and **A**stor Streets, and then **S**tuart Road.

William Owens' son, E. Alfred – the third generation in the building firm – did not want to be left out of this game and so he built **E**spin, **A**skew, **L**inton, **F**rodsham, **R**ipon, **E**mery, and **D**yson Streets.

33

GENERAL TOM THUMB IN LIVERPOOL

Phineas Taylor Barnum (1810–91) was an American showman and entrepreneur. He became famous for founding, in 1871 with his partner James Anthony Bailey (1847–1906), the internationally famous three-ring Barnum & Bailey Circus. This was advertised as being 'The Greatest Show on Earth'. However, he was particularly well known and popular as a perpetrator of publicity stunts and hoaxes, and for his ownership of the five-floor Barnum's American Museum, which he opened in New York in 1841.

This always crowded public hall of entertainment was a combination of menagerie, museum of curiosities, lecture hall, waxworks, theatre, flea circus, and 'freak' show. At its peak, the museum was open fifteen hours a day and had as many as 15,000 visitors a day.

People queued and paid to see such bizarre attractions as a loom powered by a dog, the trunk of a tree under which Jesus' disciples sat, and the Fiji Mermaid (a mummified monkey's torso with a fish's tail). Special people with physical oddities whom Barnum placed on display included dwarves, giants, fat and bearded ladies, human skeletons, the lion-faced boy, Chang and Eng the original Siamese twins, Zip the pinhead – and General Tom Thumb.

Charles Sherwood Stratton (1838–83) was born in Bridgeport, Connecticut, in the USA. He had stopped growing at the age of six months old and remained only 25in (63.5cm) tall for the rest of his life. Charles was otherwise perfectly normal, with a fully functional and proportional body.

Barnum heard about Stratton and, after contacting his parents, taught the boy how to sing, dance, mime, and impersonate famous

Phineas T. Barnum and Charles 'General Tom Thumb' Stratton. (Discover Liverpool library)

people. The showman also added the 5-year-old boy to his list of entertainers at his New York Museum. Before long, Charles had become the top attraction and was commanding a very high salary. Barnum made a great deal of money from Charles, too, but was scrupulously honest with the payments to the boy and placed them securely in trust for him.

To market the act, Barnum had given Charles the name 'General Tom Thumb', after the character in a well-known English folktale dating from 1621. Barnum took his juvenile protégé on a very successful and mutually lucrative tour of America. In specially tailored costumes, 'Tom' performed routines impersonating characters including Cupid and Napoleon Bonaparte. He also sang, danced, and had a cross-talk comedy act with a straight man.

Barnum and Charles then agreed to take the act on a worldwide tour. The first country they visited was Britain, sailing into Liverpool where, in February 1844, 'General Tom Thumb' made his first ever

British public appearance. This was for a week at the Theatre Royal in Williamson Square, with daytime celebrity appearances in the Portico Hall on Newington. (This is the narrow road that still runs between Renshaw and Bold Streets.)

Charles' fame now spread around the country. So much so that he was invited to Buckingham Palace to meet Queen Victoria and other members of the royal family. This included the future King Edward VII, who was then only 3 years old. After touring theatres around Britain with a complete supporting company, on 23rd August, 'Tom Thumb's' show returned to Liverpool. They had a six-day run of three two-hour shows per day, now at the Royal Liver Theatre, Church Street. This theatre had a capacity of almost 1,000 people, and every performance was sold out.

The Liverpool public took Charles to their hearts, and he regularly drove around the town in an open, horse-drawn carriage, waving and chatting to crowds and accepting their displays of affection and applause. He went on tour again but came back to Liverpool for more performances in the winter of 1846–47.

Charles Stratton became a very wealthy man and owned a large, specially adapted house in the fashionable part of New York, as well as a steam yacht, and an extensive wardrobe of fine clothes.

In 1863, Charles married another small show girl named Mercy Lavinia Warren, who was 32in (81cm) tall. American President Abraham Lincoln (1809–65) personally congratulated 'Tom Thumb' on his wedding and held a reception for the newlyweds at the White House. Tom and Lavinia soon became millionaires. He made his final appearance in England in 1878.

It was in 1891 that Charles 'General Tom Thumb' Stratton died, unexpectedly of a stroke. He was only 45 years old. Over 20,000 people attended his funeral and Phineas Barnum paid for a life-sized statue of 'Tom Thumb' and placed it as a grave stone at Mountain Grove Cemetery in Bridgeport, Connecticut. When she died, more than thirty-five years later, aged 77, Lavinia Warren was interred next to him with a simple grave stone that read, 'His Wife'.

34

𝕿HE 𝕵RON 𝕯UKE'S 𝕮OLUMN

The district in the heart of Liverpool that is now known as the St George's Quarter comprises one of the finest collections of neoclassical structures in Europe. These include St George's Hall (1854), the Liverpool Central Libraries (1860, restored 2013), the Walker Art Gallery (1877), and the County Sessions House (1884).

The buildings all stand along William Brown Street. This was named after the wealthy banker and slave owner who, in the mid-nineteenth century, gave the money to build the first of these stunning civic and cultural structures, Liverpool Museum (1860), now renamed the World Museum Liverpool.

At the head of the street and at the top of a hill, directly looking towards the mouth of the Queensway Mersey Tunnel at the bottom of the hill, stands a classic monument. This is the historically important and visually imposing Duke of Wellington Memorial Column. It is also known as 'The Iron Duke's Column' because of the great commander's most popular public nickname. His other common nickname, especially among his troops – but always used with affection – was 'Conky Bill', because of his great hooked nose!

The column is mounted on a stepped plinth and was erected as a tribute to Arthur Wellesley, the 1st Duke of Wellington (1769–1852), who was one of Britain's greatest national heroes. This was particularly because of his victory over the French Emperor Napoleon Bonaparte (1769–1821) at the Battle of Waterloo in 1815, in what is now Belgium.

Wellesley was known by the public as 'the Iron Duke' because of his determination and formidable resolve, and he had been prime minister of Britain from 1823 to 1830, and again in 1834. He was a trusted advisor to a young Queen Victoria (1819–1901), and after his

Unveiling the Iron Duke's Column. (Liverpool Athenaeum library)

death the people of Liverpool wished to honour the memory of this outstanding military leader.

The fluted column was designed by Andrew Lawson from Glasgow and its foundation stone was laid in 1861. The monument was formally unveiled on 16 May 1863, in front of an appreciative and enthusiastic crowd of thousands of people. As the Iron Duke's statue was revealed, a salvo was fired from nineteen cannon, followed by a band playing 'Hail The Conquering Hero Comes'.

Standing 132ft (40m) high, the Wellington column was carved from Darleydale stone and supports a bronze statue of the duke. This figure was designed by Andrew Lawson's brother, George, and is 14ft (4m) high. It is cast in metal that was melted down from cannon captured from the French at Waterloo.

The statue is positioned facing south-east, so that Wellington will always be looking towards the site of what had been his greatest military victory. A brass panel relief at the base of the column shows the final charge at Waterloo, and the duke can be seen mounted on his horse, telescope in hand, commanding the advance against the enemy. On the east and west faces of the pedestal, other panels, mounted in

1865, list the names of the duke's other victorious battles. The east panel records Assaye, Talavera, Argaum, Busaco, Rolica, Fuentes de Onoro, Vimeiro, Cuidad Rodrigo, Oporto, and Badajoz; and the west panel lists the battles of Salamanca, Bayonne, Vittoria, Orthez, San Sebastian, Toulouse, Nivelle, Quatre Bras, and Waterloo.

The column is, in fact, a hollow cylinder, inside which a spiral stone staircase of 169 steps travels up to a viewing platform below the duke. Though cemented onto the column, the statue is also secured in place by a thick steel cable. This is kept under tension and anchored at the base of the monument.

A recently rediscovered tunnel leads from the basement of St George's Hall, under Lime Street, directly to a cellar beneath the column. This gives access to the steps to the top.

Another curious feature is what is set into the base of the column's surrounding pavement. These are the pre-metric, Imperial Standard, Board of Trade measurements of length at 62 degrees Fahrenheit. The shorter ones, at 1in, 1ft, and 1 yard, are mounted onto a bronze panel fixed to an adjacent wall. From this, set into the pavement and running parallel with the nearby Walker Art Gallery, is set a long, brass strip. This shows the larger measures of 100ft (30m), and a chain of a 100 links.

The Wellington column fits in perfectly with the other statuary, monuments, and buildings that together make up the St George's Quarter. This whole area of the city centre reveals just how the mid-Victorian leaders of Liverpool regarded their town as a 'New Rome' and themselves as latter-day classical 'senators'.

35

LIVERPOOL'S TITANIC MEMORIALS

When it was built at the Harland & Wolff shipyard in Belfast, RMS *Titanic* was the largest ship afloat, standing as high as an eleven-storey building. She was owned by the Liverpool-based White Star Line and was Liverpool registered, although she never visited the city.

On 10 April 1912, the huge luxury transatlantic passenger liner set sail with over 2,200 passengers and crew on board. This was her maiden voyage from Southampton to New York, via Queenstown (now Cobh) in Ireland. At 11.40 p.m. on the night of 14 April 1912, she struck an iceberg just off Cape Race in the North Atlantic. She eventually sank at 2.20 a.m. on the morning of Monday, 15 April, with the loss of 1,490 lives.

Even today, the magnitude of this disaster resonates clearly, particularly as it was so completely avoidable. It is likely that the ship had been travelling too fast to avoid the iceberg, but the vessel actually took so long to go down that everybody could have survived – if there had been sufficient lifeboats. However, during the design stage, the White Star Line felt not only that the extra lifeboats would clutter up the decks, but that as the vessel was unsinkable, they could save a great deal of money by having only a minimal number on board.

This view was endorsed by the British Board of Trade, which confirmed that twenty lifeboats with a capacity of 1,178 places was perfectly acceptable. Even though all the lifeboats were successfully launched as the vessel began to slowly sink, this staggering lack of capacity meant that only 705 people were rescued. Perhaps predictably, considering the class-governed culture of the time, there were more first-class male survivors than third-class child survivors.

Of those passengers and crew who could not get aboard a lifeboat, yet managed to get into the sea safely, most of these died because the waters of the North Atlantic were so intolerably freezing, rather than by drowning. So, when the rescue vessels did eventually arrive it was far too late to save these men, women, children, and babies. All they found were frozen corpses, wearing lifebelts and bobbing about in the calm but icy waters. The rest is history.

There are two memorials to the *Titanic* disaster in Liverpool, and one of these is at the Pier Head, between the Liver Building and the Crowne Plaza Hotel. This is an obelisk, built as a result of the disaster and erected following a public subscription. It was unveiled in 1916.

This was originally intended to be a memorial to the thirty-two engineers who stayed at their posts aboard *Titanic* on that fateful night. However, the First World War broke out before it was completed and so the dedication was broadened. It is now dedicated as a general memorial to all engineers and stokers who have lost their lives at sea. As such, it is officially called the Memorial to the Engine Room Heroes. However, it will always be known locally as 'The *Titanic* Memorial' and it attracts much attention because of this association.

On one side of the obelisk are depicted two stokers standing in front of a furnace door. On the opposite side, two officers holding tools stand in front of a telegraph. On the four corners are the

The Memorial to the Engine Room Heroes at Liverpool's Pier Head. (Discover Liverpool library)

symbols of earth, air, fire, and water and, at the top, below a symbolic eternal fame, stand four figures holding lifebelts. An inscription reads,

> The brave do not die,
> their deeds live for ever and call upon us
> to emulate their courage and devotion to duty.

None of the engineers or engineering officers survived from *Titanic*. Every man stayed at his post almost until the great ship sank beneath the Atlantic. They kept the boilers stoked and fired and the ship's lights burning, in the vain hope of attracting rescue ships in time to save everybody aboard.

The second memorial to the *Titanic* disaster is dedicated to the ship's band. This can be found in the foyer of the Philharmonic Hall on Hope Street, and it lists the names of all the musicians. They each continued to play as the ship began to sink, and their last melody is now believed to have been the popular melody 'Autumn', rather than the hymn 'Nearer My God To Thee' of popular belief.

However, it is noteworthy that another memorial to this catastrophe stands in our sister seafaring town of Southampton. It was from here that many of the crew of the vessel were recruited and, of these, 637 people died, completely devastating the community. But many families in Liverpool lost relatives among the crew also. Indeed, so many of the crew came from the Vauxhall area of Liverpool that the main gangway in the crew quarters aboard *Titanic* was nicknamed 'Scotland Road' after one of the long main roads in that district.

As a footnote, on 1 September 1985, a Franco-American expedition led by Dr Robert Ballard, discovered and photographed *Titanic* lying, as it now does, on the ocean floor 12,460ft (3.8km) below the surface of the North Atlantic Ocean. Since that time, the tragic remains of one of the world's greatest maritime disasters continue to be the subject of much scientific investigation, attempted plundering by treasure seekers and souvenir hunters, and a destination for wealthy, well-equipped, underwater tourists. However, what seems to be all too easily ignored is the fact that this is the grave site of over 1,500 people.

36

𝔓ISTOLS AT 𝔇AWN

In the early nineteenth century, what became known as 'The Dingle Duel' was the penultimate such gunfight in Liverpool – and it was a local sensation.

In the early morning of Friday, 24 February 1804, the scene was to be set in the secluded groves of the Dingle. This was once a rural area of detached mansions, surrounded by acres of bluebell woods, rhododendrons, linden trees, and wildflowers. It was all set on top of a rocky outcropping in Toxteth, overlooking the River Mersey and Wirral.

As the cold sun rose on that late winter's morning, the Dingle Brook and other streams skipped and gurgled their merry, dancing ways across the almost Arcadian setting. The trees and shrubberies were already filled with birdsong, and their branches were breaking up the early sunlight into a carpet of mottled, shimmering gold on the grass beneath. The Dingle had been described as being 'A paradise in the North ... One of the most beautiful places in the district ... a sweet, romantic dell, planted and laid out with considerable taste', but this tranquillity was about to be brutally shattered.

Mr William Sparling, of St Domingo House, Everton, a lieutenant in the 10th Regiment of Dragoons, and Mr Edward Grayson, an eminent shipbuilder, met outside the ancient chapel of Toxteth, at 7.00 a.m. (as you will read later in this book, this chapel dates from the seventeenth century and still stands at the end of Park Road in Toxteth). It was only a matter of a few hundred yards away from where this duel was to be fought.

The cause of the argument was a reported conversation in which Grayson called Sparling 'a villain' for breaking off the marriage between himself and a relative of Grayson's. Sparling did not get the apology and retraction that he had demanded from Grayson, so the challenge had been issued and accepted.

The duellists' seconds were carrying pistol cases, but no words were exchanged as the antagonists' servants saw to their respective master's immediate needs. The duellists and their seconds made their way into the woodlands and quickly disappeared from the sight of their servants. They remained with the carriages on Park Road, together with Dr McCartney, who had been brought to attend to any injuries.

Almost immediately, and without warning, shots were heard. Grayson's servant ran into the groves with the doctor, meeting Sparling and his second, Captain Colquitt, coming the other way.

'Your master is wounded, you had best attend him,' said Sparling, as he and his second got into their carriage and drove back into town. Grayson's servant found his master lying prone and clearly in great pain. His breeches were soaked through with blood.

The critically wounded man was carried back to his carriage and taken at all speed back to his home. On the journey, Dr McCartney attempted, without success, to stem the copious flow of blood. Grayson lingered until the following Sunday, when he died.

Mr Sparling and Captain Colquitt were accused of murder at the inquest, and tried at Lancaster assizes on 4 April. Without consulting the jury, in his summing up, the presiding judge, Sir Alan Cambre, simply leaned towards the prisoners in the dock and declared sonorously, 'Not guilty!'

The last duel in Liverpool was fought the following year, in 1805. This was between Colonel John Bolton and Major Edward Brooks.

John Bolton was born in Ulverston, Cumbria, in 1756, and traded in the West Indies before settling in Liverpool around 1790. A staunch patriot, in 1797 he contributed £500 (£48,665 today) to a committee set up to defend Liverpool after French troops had landed at Fishguard. He then set up his own Liverpool Volunteers in 1803, at his own expense. Becoming known as the Bolton Invincibles, they trained at Mosslake Fields, near Edge Hill in Liverpool.

In 1804 Major Edward Brooks, who was a 'customs jerker' (an officer who searches vessels for undeclared goods), asked for a wage increase. Bolton, who, as president of the West India Association, was

Pistols at dawn to settle an argument, once and for all. (Discover Liverpool library)

his boss, refused, saying that Brooks was paid enough already. The customs officer immediately challenged his employer to a duel, which was accepted. The date was agreed as 20 December that same year, the venue to be Millers Dam, a small, secluded creek on Aigburth Road, not far from Otterspool (of which more later).

The men arrived, with seconds and servants, at the appointed early hour but were immediately arrested by local constables. Someone had anonymously tipped off the authorities. Bolton and Brooks were both bound over to keep the peace for a year. However, Brooks, who was described as being a person with 'a great amount of irritable vanity and pugnacity', would not let the matter rest.

Over the next twelve months Brooks kept issuing threats and insults about Bolton at every available opportunity. Then, exactly one year after their first abortive duel, in fact, on 20 December 1805, Brooks publicly insulted Bolton to his face, on Castle Street in the town. Indeed, he 'called him by a name which no gentleman could put up with'.

Brooks was immediately arrested for a few hours, but immediately upon his release he issued a new challenge to his enemy. Bolton was forced to accept this, just to put the matter to rest.

Darkness was falling by the time both men arrived, this time at a field near what is now Pembroke Place in the city. They were again both accompanied by seconds and servants, and by Mr Park, a local surgeon. Pistols had to be checked and loaded by lamplight as daylight had now faded, then both men walked their ten paces away from each other. The duellists immediately turned towards each other and Brooks fired the first shot. He missed. Bolton then returned fire and killed Brooks outright by putting his pistol ball directly through his opponent's eye.

There being no mortuary or hospital in the vicinity at that time, Brooks' body had to be temporarily stored in the beer cellar of the Albert Pub in Lark Lane, Aigburth. Bolton went into hiding for a short while and the inquest found him guilty of murder. However, due to public opinion being behind him, and the fact he had been belligerently challenged by Brooks, he was never charged.

Bolton remained in Liverpool political life until his death in 1837. Bolton Street, which runs directly behind Lime Street, is named after him.

37

THE BONEYARD: ST JOHN'S ORNAMENTAL AND MEMORIAL GARDENS

The delightful gardens that now stand to the rear of St George's Hall were originally, and from 1767, the Liverpool town cemetery. This stood on what was then the extreme eastern edge of what was still a relatively small, but growing, community. The cemetery was known locally as 'the Boneyard' and consisted of ranks of graves and tombs plus a large pit with a removable lid, for the regular burial of paupers, vagrants, and criminals. People tended to avoid this if possible as the stench from it was dreadful!

With the sudden rapid expansion of the town's geography and population from the mid-1700s, a new church was needed, so it was built in the centre of the burial ground. This was St John the Baptist Church and it opened in 1784.

As we have seen, from 1799 to 1815, Britain was fighting the Napoleonic Wars and had captured thousands of French soldiers and sailors as prisoners of war. During the war, and for some years afterwards, 4,000 of these poor unfortunates were held in Liverpool. But we had been holding French prisoners from captured privateers and French revolutionary ships for at least twenty years before this.

The unfortunate men were first confined in the squalid dungeons and cells of the notorious medieval Tower of Liverpool, and later in the overcrowded cells of the Borough Gaol, which had opened in 1786. Conditions were so appalling in both prisons that, by 1803, around 230 Frenchmen had died from combinations of typhus (also known as jail fever), starvation, and brutality. A second pit was kept for the unceremonious burial of these bodies, in a corner of the Boneyard.

The population of the town had grown so much that, by 1854, the cemetery was full with around 82,500 corpses. It was closed later that year but the church was in use until around 1890. However, this was demolished in 1898. The remains of most of the bodies were then removed from the graveyard and buried elsewhere.

By this time, St George's Hall had been built (in 1841), and it was decided that, as an attractive backdrop to the magnificent and stately civic building, the former graveyard should be landscaped. The site was then redeveloped, and opened in 1904 as St John's Ornamental and Memorial Gardens.

However, when the graveyard was closed, the French bodies were the only ones not removed with dignity. Their bones were simply dug

The rather obscure burial site plaque for the French prisoners, set into the rear wall of St John's Memorial Gardens. (Discover Liverpool library)

up and packed into a new vault. This is set into the rear wall of the gardens and below the pathway, above which runs St George's Hall.

In 1924, on Armistice Day, a commemorative plaque was unveiled. It reads:

To her sons who died in captivity in Liverpool 1772–1803,
and whose bodies lie here in the old cemetery of St. John the Baptist.
France ever grateful.

This plaque is mounted on the wall directly over the French burial vault – and the bones are still there. France actually has little to be grateful for, I would have thought!

There are six principal memorial statues in the gardens, commemorating some of Liverpool's leading men of the past. No women though (yet), despite their many accomplishments.

The Rathbone Monument commemorates William Rathbone VI, MP and philanthropist, who died in 1902. The Gladstone Monument is to the memory of W.E. Gladstone, a former prime minister, who was born in Liverpool and who died in 1898. The Balfour Monument commemorates Alexander Balfour, businessman and philanthropist, who died in 1886.

The Lester Monument is to the memory of Canon Major Thomas Lester, who founded charities for children in Liverpool and died in 1903. The Nugent Memorial commemorates Father James Nugent, a Roman Catholic priest, who worked with child welfare. The Forwood Monument is to the memory of Sir Arthur Forwood, a local businessman and politician, who died in 1898.

The most powerful monument, however, stands in the centre of the gardens and is dedicated to the men of Liverpool who, for centuries, have served and sacrificed as soldiers of the King's Liverpool Regiment. This bronze group was sculpted by Sir William Goscombe John and was unveiled in 1905. The lifelike figures are commanding, and I find the expression on the face of the young drummer boy to be especially telling.

St John's is truly a memorial garden, with special plots and sculptures dedicated to many groups, including:

The Holocaust Memorial
All Victims of Persecution
Victims of Road Accidents
RAF Memorial
Alder Hey Children's Hospital
The Burma Star
The Cheshire Regiment
The Eighth Army
The Irish Guards
The Korean War
The Northern Ireland Conflicts
The Normandy Landings (D-Day)
The Parachute Regiment
Victims of the Hiroshima and Nagasaki Bombings
The Queen's Lancashire Regiment
The Royal Green Jackets
The Scots Guards
World AIDS Day
British Nuclear Test Victims
Families Fighting for Justice
The Heysel Stadium Disaster
The Liverpool CVS Plaque
The Royal Corps of Signals
Rwanda Genocide

Just outside the western wall to the gardens stands one of Liverpool's
four memorials to the victims of the 1989 Hillsborough football
stadium disaster, where ninety-five adults and children were crushed
to death. Of course, many hundreds of people were severely injured,
many having their lives drastically changed forever. One of these
was Hillsborough's ninety-sixth victim, Tony Bland, who suffered
irreparable brain damage in the crush and died in 1993. The most
recent person to be killed by Hillsborough was Andrew Stanley
Devine. He sadly passed away in July 2021, at the age of 55, as a result
of his injuries at Hillsborough. Andrew became the disaster's ninety-
seventh victim.

38

THE RAILWAYS AND THE ROCKET

The Industrial Revolution of the late eighteenth and early nineteenth centuries irrevocably changed the face of Britain. However, the construction in Liverpool of the very first passenger railway was another revolution of immense significance for the town, for Britain, and for the world.

There were already a number of railway lines in Britain in the early decades of the nineteenth century, but these were mostly for industrial purposes, such as hauling coal and other goods over short distances in collieries, and most of these were horse drawn. However, this all changed when the great engineer George Stephenson (1781–1848) was invited to come to Liverpool by certain wealthy and prominent businessmen from the town, and from nearby Manchester. These men were the directors of the new Liverpool & Manchester Railway Company (L&MR), and they proposed to build a railway powered by some form of steam engine.

This revolutionary transportation system would provide faster movement of raw materials and finished goods, as well as passengers (although this was an afterthought), between the port of Liverpool and the cotton mills of Manchester. Road and canal transport were no longer efficient or fast enough for the ambitions of these men in this modern age. Also, they felt that a railway would be cheaper to run and more profitable.

The new link between the two great northern cities would be the very first, true, twin-track passenger steam locomotive to run anywhere in the world. They knew that Stephenson and his son Robert (1803–59) would be equal to this great technical challenge and, in 1826, the engineers came to Liverpool and set to work.

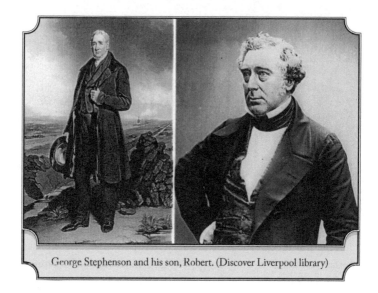

George Stephenson and his son, Robert. (Discover Liverpool library)

The line would consist of two parallel tracks covering a distance of 35 miles, which would have to be laid over some very difficult terrain, including the treacherous Chat Moss. This 12-mile-square expanse of soggy bog, in places 40ft (12.2m) deep, lies 5 miles west of Manchester, directly on the route between the two cities.

Stephenson eventually decided to 'float' his line across it, by distributing the load over a wide surface. This was specially prepared by laying sand, earth, and gravel, thickly coated with cinders, upon overlapping hurdles of branches, heather, and brushwood. Modern trains still run over Stephenson's imaginative foundations.

However, this was not the only significant engineering problem that Stephenson had to overcome. The line began with a goods depot at Wapping Dock in Liverpool, then travelled through a 2,250-yard tunnel beneath Liverpool to Crown Street Station at Edge Hill. Here, passengers boarded trains to and from Manchester. (The construction of Lime Street Station, in the heart of Liverpool, did not happen until 1836.) From Edge Hill, the line then ran through a 2-mile cutting, at one point up to 70ft (21.3m) deep, through solid sandstone bedrock at Olive Mount in Wavertree.

Then a viaduct had to cross over the Sankey Brook Valley, supported by nine 50ft (15.2m) wide arches, each around 70ft (21.3m) high. Also, numerous massive embankments and other cuttings had to be constructed along the route.

All of these magnificent feats of civil engineering were carried out, using only muscle power, by George Stephenson's labourers. These men were known as navvies, because many of them had already dug many of Britain's canals, known colloquially as 'navigations'.

In 1828, the railway directors could not agree on how to power their new transportation system, and so they decided to hold a competitive series of railway trials to choose the most effective locomotive. These had to take place quickly as work on the tracks was now well under way. And so, beginning on 8 October 1829, at Rainhill just outside Liverpool, a number of locomotives were to compete against each other, not just for the contract, but for a prize of £500 (£42,500).

While George was largely occupied in supervising the building of the railway line, he had every intention of winning the Rainhill Steam Trials using his son Robert's locomotive on his own railway tracks. His son, who was then only 24 years of age, was more than equal to the task. He concentrated on developing their entry for the competition, the *Rocket*, which was one of five locomotives being tested. The others were *Novelty*, built by Messrs Braithewaite and Ericsson of London; *Perseverance*, built by Mr Burstall of Edinburgh; and *Sans Pariel*, built by Mr Hackworth of Darlington. Each of these were steam powered. There was also the *Cycloped*, built by Dr Brandreth of Liverpool. However, this was disqualified because it was powered by a tethered horse and jockey on a treadmill!

Competitors had to run their locomotives ten times in each direction over a 1½-mile course. After a break to take on water and fuel, another ten runs had to be completed, each of which were timed. George and Robert Stephenson won the rigorous trials in grand style, having attached a coach to their engine containing thirty passengers. Not only was their engine the most scientifically advanced engine at that time, but it also looked good with its tall smokestack and brightly painted bodywork.

They further impressed the judges, spectators, and no doubt their passengers, by travelling at the impossible speed of between 24 and

30mph! This was twice the speed of even the fastest stagecoach and defied the common belief that people would not be able to breathe at such speeds. At the conclusion of the trials, *Rocket* was the only locomotive to have completed the course and so was declared the outright winner. The £500 prize was duly awarded to the Stephensons.

Following the contest, the fame and popularity of the locomotive was almost universal and the construction of the world's first inter-city passenger railway could forge ahead, ready for its opening on 15 September 1830. This revolutionary form of transport would change the world forever.

39

THE ANGEL OF THE SLUMS

The second person I want to tell of in this book, who undoubtedly put others before themselves and at great personal sacrifice, was Catherine 'Kitty' Seaward (1786–1860).

Kitty was a very ordinary woman indeed, but one who achieved extraordinary things. In fact, she had been born in Ireland into a poor family.

In 1794, when she was 11 years old, Kitty's parents decided to leave their home and travel, with her and her young brother and baby sister, to the important and growing seaport of Liverpool, far across the Irish Sea. Kitty's father knew that there would be work there for them all, so there was a chance that they could find a better life for themselves. In those days, of course, even children went out to work and only wealthy children went to school.

So, they scrimped and saved until they had enough money to pay for tickets on the large sailing ship that would carry them overseas. They did not have much money and could only afford places on the deck of the ship, exposed to the waves, wind, and rain. Nevertheless, with their hearts full of hopes and dreams, they set sail.

The voyage began well but on the second day, and without warning, the sky turned dark and the wind began to blow up into a gale. The waves began to rise and thrash about the ship and, before long, a great storm filled the sky and whipped up the seas. Soon, the ship was tossing and tipping as the waves grew higher, and as the strong winds screamed through the rigging and howled across the great, flapping sails, tearing huge shreds off them'.

Kitty's family huddled together in a corner of the deck when, suddenly, an enormous, towering wave of cold, grey water crashed right over the ship and onto the terrified people. Then Kitty's father was gone. He had been washed overboard.

The storm raged on but, just as people thought that the ship was about to sink, it ran aground on a sandbank not far from the Wirral coast. Fortunately, a lifeboat rowed out to them.

Soon, Kitty, with her little brother and their mother, who still held the baby in her arms, found themselves being helped down the side of the ship into the lifeboat. But, just at that moment, a sudden gust of strong wind blew across them and the baby was swept from her mother's arms by the

Kitty Wilkinson, the Angel of the Slums. (Liverpool Athenaeum library)

gale, also to be washed into the sea, never to be seen again.

And so, of this poor little Irish family, only Kitty, her mother, and her small brother made it safely to Liverpool. As well as their father and the baby, they had lost most of their belongings. They only had enough money left to rent a small room in a crowded house, in one of the poorest parts of the town.

Kitty, still only 11 years old, and her mother now had to immediately find work to buy food and pay the rent. A kindly neighbour looked after Kitty's small brother while they worked as servants for very long hours and for very little pay.

In eighteenth- and nineteenth-century Liverpool the streets were narrow, dark, and heavily overcrowded. In the terraced and back-to-back houses, tenements, and court dwellings in the slum areas, two or three families often shared a single room. There might be five, six, or even seven families living in each dwelling, even in the cellars and the attics. There was little or no light and no fresh air.

This was before the days of pipes and plumbing, so there was no supply of fresh water for people to drink, except perhaps from filthy streams that ran past the buildings or from the occasional water pump or well. This also meant that there was no way that anyone could properly wash themselves, their clothes, bed sheets or blankets. People were generally filthy and the smell must have been awful.

There were no sewers or proper lavatories for people to use, except for holes in the ground inside small, wooden toilet cubicles, mostly without doors or roofs. These stood at the ends of the open streets, passages, or courtyards, and were shared by everybody. Otherwise, they just urinated and defecated wherever they could!

It was in conditions like these that Kitty and her family had to live. Nevertheless, the girl and her brother grew up, although their mother grew quite ill and eventually died.

When she was 25, Kitty met and married a man called Tom Wilkinson, and this was a happy match. Tom had regular work and so he and Kitty were able to rent a bigger house, with a lot of rooms. They also bought a very big copper boiler, heated by a fire and in which she could do laundry. This meant that Kitty could earn the odd penny or two by doing the washing for her neighbours. However, they still lived in the poorer part of town and had little money to spare.

Then, in 1832, there was an outbreak of cholera. This quickly swept through the overcrowded, dingy, dark and damp slum streets, houses, and cellars of Liverpool. It killed over 1,500 people, mostly old people, children, and babies.

Kitty and Tom did what they could to alleviate the suffering of their neighbours and friends. The young woman, in particular, began to nurse the sick people in the streets around her home, and she also cooked soup in her kitchen and gave it away to the needy. She and Tom also opened their home up to anyone who needed care or shelter, free of charge.

But the cholera continued to sweep through the districts, killing hundreds of people.

This was a time when people's knowledge of essential health and hygiene was either non-existent or only rudimentary. Even so, Kitty knew enough to recognise that dirt and filth caused the illness to spread. She realised, too, that if people could drink clean water, could be careful where and how they went to the toilet, and could keep themselves and their clothes and bedding clean, then the cholera might stop.

The young Irishwoman now began to take in loads of her neighbours' soiled clothes and bedding. She washed them in her great copper boiler, only charging a penny a time from those that could afford it, but mostly doing it for free. She also taught people how to wash and bathe themselves and their children, and allowed them to do this in hot water from her boiler too! Soon, in the neighbourhoods around Kitty's house, the disease began to disappear and sick people were beginning to recover. Everyone in her neighbourhood knew that this was because of Kitty and her 'wash house' in her home, and she was respected and loved by the people.

Soon, the leaders of the town heard what Kitty was doing. They visited Kitty and Tom to learn for themselves. As a result, they quickly spent money on building public washhouses all over the town and public baths too. These could be used by anyone for only a couple of pennies. Indeed, Kitty and Tom were employed as managers in the very first of these, in Frederick Street.

Over the coming years, Liverpool Corporation employed public health workers and doctors. They also installed a clean, piped water supply throughout the town. They built proper roads and began demolishing all the slum houses. They also built the first council housing estates in Britain in the town, each with their own taps and fresh water supply, and with proper outside lavatories for everyone, connected to a brand-new sewer system.

When she died in 1860 at the age of 75, Kitty was buried in St James' Cemetery at the foot of the Anglican cathedral in town, where her grave can still be seen. In fact, crowds of people turned out to her funeral, to pay their respects to this very ordinary but very special woman. She had been determined to help others and to make a difference – in her own very ordinary way.

Kitty has a commemorative window in the Lady Chapel of Liverpool Anglican cathedral, and a marble statue of her was unveiled, inside St George's Hall, in 2012. Simply by washing clothes, and people, she changed Liverpool forever, and we all live healthier and cleaner lives because of Kitty Wilkinson, 'The Angel of the Slums'.

40

ℕEGLECTED 𝕎OOLTON ℍALL

Liverpool is fortunate in that we still have quite a number of stately homes and mansions within the city and throughout its suburbs. Croxteth Hall, the home of the Molyneux family, the Viscounts and Earls of Sefton, is now owned by Liverpool City Council. The house and grounds are fully open to the public.

Then we have Speke Hall, at the extreme south of the city. This beautiful, timber-framed, moated mansion, with four wings around a central courtyard, is recognised as being one of the finest examples of Jacobean architecture in Britain. This is now in the care of the National Trust.

The very large and quite magnificent Knowsley Hall stands to the east of Liverpool in the suburb of West Derby. This remains the private, ancestral residence of the Earls of Derby. Currently, the 19th Earl and Countess reside there with their family, and the building and large estate are only opened to the public once a year for a limited time, unless one is visiting Knowsley Safari Park.

Lots of other former grand mansions are now hotels, nursing homes, conference centres, and student halls of residence. A few others, however, have been abandoned by their former (or even current owners) and allowed to fall into dereliction and decay. One such is Woolton Hall. This is a house with a fascinating past and could well be facing a grim future.

The suburb of Woolton is one of Liverpool's many lost villages and has Anglo-Saxon origins. The manor of Woolton was owned by the Knights of St John of Jerusalem (Knights Hospitallers) from around 1180. Queen Elizabeth I owned it from 1559, Robert of Upholland in 1609, then King James I.

William Stanley, 6th Earl of Derby, was a later lord of Woolton manor, followed by the wealthy lawyer and landowner from Prescot,

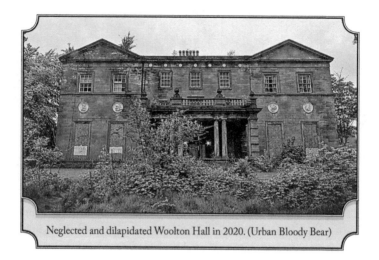

Neglected and dilapidated Woolton Hall in 2020. (Urban Bloody Bear)

Isaac Greene. He went on to also own the manors of Allerton, Mossley Hill, Gateacre, Childwall, West Derby, Wavertree, Everton and, through marriage, the township of Hale.

Woolton and the rest of Green's holdings then passed to Bamber Gascoigne of Childwall Hall. From him, the manor eventually came into the hands of the Marquesses of Salisbury. The current lord of Woolton and the rest of Isaac Green's manors (except Hale) is Robert Michael James Gascoyne-Cecil, 7th Marquess of Salisbury, Baron Gascoyne-Cecil (b.1946).

During the Tudor era, what would evolve into Woolton village's stately home, Woolton Hall, was held by the Brettargh family of Brettargh Holt near Gateacre. They owned what is now much of Gateacre, Lee Park, and Netherley. They are said to have acquired the original house from an even older family named de Woolton. Then, sometime after 1609, the original hall and estate passed from the Brettarghs.

In 1704, the ancient building became the property of William, 4th Viscount Molyneux (1655–1717). He pulled down the house and built the core of the Woolton Hall that we have today. Eventually becoming the Earls of Sefton in 1771, this family held the hall until 1772.

It was in this year that it was acquired by Nicholas Ashton (1742–1833), a former high sheriff of Lancashire. His father, John Ashton

(1711–59), was one of the founders of the Sankey Canal, the first canal of the British Industrial Revolution. The family were also involved in the salt trade at Hale and Speke, in coal mining at St Helens, and they profited considerably from the slave trade.

From around 1746, Nicholas, in partnership with John Blackburne (1754–1833), of Blackburne House in Liverpool, owned a salt refinery in the small community of Dungeon, near Speke. Salt mined in Cheshire was brought down the Mersey from Widnes to Dungeon on barges and flat boats. The refined salt was then carried on more flat boats to the South Dock, in central Liverpool. Here, it was stored in a long, low, wooden warehouse on the quayside, named the Salthouse. The dock soon became known as the Salthouse Dock, which it is still called today.

The salt was sold principally to preserve food at sea, in the days before refrigeration. Dungeon salt also found its way to the cod fisheries of Newfoundland. Huge quantities of fish were then preserved there to be shipped to the Caribbean. This was then fed to the slaves on the sugar, coffee, indigo, and rice plantations. Hundreds of slaves were owned by Ashton and Blackburne.

In 1772, Nicholas Ashton commissioned the noted architect Robert Adam (1728–92) to remodel and expand Woolton Hall extensively – largely as we see it today. From 1865, the hall's next owner was American entrepreneur James Reddecliffe Jeffery.

In 1832, with his brother William, James opened one of Liverpool's largest department stores, Compton House, standing on Church Street. All of his 180 staff were resident and lived in the upper floors.

In 1865, a fire destroyed the building, but the insurance money enabled the brothers to rebuild it as the Compton Hotel. There was enough money left over from the insurance claim to allow James to buy and refurbish Woolton Hall. Compton Hotel reopened in 1867, and by 1930 had become the flagship Marks & Spencer's department store.

From 1877, Woolton Hall was owned by Sir Frederick Leyland (1831–92). He was a wealthy ship owner and art collector, who had moved, with his family from their previous home at Speke Hall.

From 1902 to around 1912, the owner was Captain Andrew McGuffie. He too was a ship owner. He demolished the west wing and converted the building into a hydropathic hotel, with an adjoining nine-hole golf course. Here, his patrons could not only play a round, but also take hot mineral baths and drink sulphurous mineral water, bake in a steam cabinet, receive dynamic enemas (whatever those are!), undergo cold high-pressure hosings, and also risk electrocution in a hydroelectric bath. Among McGuffie's patrons were the American Consul, and successful local biscuit manufacturer Alexander Crawford. However, after a few years the novelty of these exotic treatments wore off and the Woolton Hall Hydro Hotel closed in 1912.

After a short spell as the headquarters of the Middlesex Regiment and as an army hospital, the building was converted into a fee-paying girls' school, under the management of the nuns of the Convent of Notre Dame. But then the building was left abandoned by the nuns and for a short time operated as a function suite and conference venue. This did not last though, and Woolton Hall was earmarked for demolition in the 1980s.

Fortunately, the building was saved after local resident John Hibbert purchased the hall and spent £100,000 on refurbishment. On 28 June 1982, Woolton Hall become a Grade-I-listed building.

In 2005, there were plans to convert the estate and house into retirement care flats but this didn't happen. There was also a major fire in 2019, which caused significant damage both inside and outside. Tragically, and despite its heritage listing and historic significance, Woolton Hall still stands empty, closed up, and often vandalised. In February 2021, the current owner put the hall on the market, the asking price was £4 million. At the time of writing, it remains unsold, and the future is not looking optimistic. However, local campaigns to save the Hall, and put it to appropriate and self-sustaining use, are energetic and determined – so all is not yet lost.

41

𝕿HE 𝕿RUE 𝕴NVENTOR OF 𝕽ADIO?

Perhaps it was not Marconi who invented radio …

There is strong evidence that the first transmission and reception of a radio signal took place in Oxford University, demonstrated by Sir Oliver Lodge. He was born in 1851, and went on to become a renowned scientist and professor at the University of Liverpool.

Sir Oliver was elected the first Professor of Physics at University College, Liverpool, in June 1881 and was a pioneer in wireless. He researched and developed electromagnetism and the nature and propagation of radio waves.

In 1888, he produced the first electromagnetic waves around wires. In 1889, he devised the first selective tuner to receive and strengthen radio signals, and he named this process 'syntony'. He patented this discovery in 1897, and if you have ever tuned in a radio, then you have used Sir Oliver Lodge's invention.

While he was a professor at Liverpool in 1894, he devised a very sensitive radio wave receiver, which he called a 'coherer'. This was the first practical radio receiver or 'wireless'. It was in this same year, on 14 August, that he sent his very first radio message. This was transmitted from the Clarendon Laboratory in Oxford – a distance of 180ft (60m) through two stone walls – to the Oxford Museum lecture theatre, with a scientific audience of members of the British Association.

Following this achievement, Sir Oliver's next radio transmission was in 1897, from the top of the Liverpool University Clocktower, in the Victoria Building on Brownlow Hill. This was sent to a receiver on the roof of Lewis's Store at the bottom of Brownlow Hill – a distance of about half a mile.

Sir Oliver Lodge, the true inventor of radio.
(Liverpool Athenaeum library)

He began to send regular wireless messages to his wife from the Clocktower – this was as he was about to set off for home from his university office, telling her when to have his tea ready! However, he got into trouble with the authorities because his radio signals were setting off all sorts of fire and burglar alarms in the vicinity, so he had to stop.

Then, in 1898, Sir Oliver designed and patented the moving-coil loudspeaker. This was very important because without it we would never have had hi-fi radio or record decks, and everything that developed from these.

The Italian inventor, Guglielmo Marconi (1874–1937) is given the honour of being the inventor of radio, but his part in its development was actually the transmission of a radio message from a ship at sea to a shore station, which did not take place until 1901. However, the ability to call for assistance in a time of peril was indeed a truly magnificent achievement by Marconi, and this immediately caught the imagination of the public, governments, and the business world.

The success of this first ship-to-shore transmission and the reception of a radio signal was well publicised because Marconi saw to the worldwide promotion himself. He was already a wealthy man, who could easily afford to advertise himself and his 'invention of radio', which wasn't really his invention at all. As a result, Marconi went on to establish a very successful worldwide company.

Sir Oliver Lodge, however, who really looked the part of a Victorian scientist, with a high forehead, bald dome, and long, white beard, was more interested in research than in making money. He went on to make many more significant discoveries, and to contribute to effective scientific research and development for many years, before he died in 1940.

You can easily see what Sir Oliver Lodge looked like because he was the model for the scientist shown in the bronze sculpture group named 'Learning', at the base of the Queen Victoria Monument in Derby Square, at the top of Lord Street in Liverpool.

42

BONNIE PRINCE CHARLIE'S CHAIR

In the English Civil War (1642–51), Liverpool town was besieged three times, changing hands between the Roundheads and the Cavaliers. As mentioned previously in this book, in 1644, Prince Rupert of the Rhine, the 24-year-old nephew of King Charles I, came here to capture Liverpool. We saw how he commandeered a cottage on a street named Browside, in the heart of Everton village. He used this as his HQ, and from here he looked down on the tiny town and declared that it was no more than 'A nest of crows that a parcel of boys could take!' Ever afterwards, the building was known as 'Prince Rupert's Cottage'. But that is another story entirely!

As we have also seen, there are a number of fascinating fables and tales associated with Everton village, one of which comes from the Jacobite Rebellion of 1745. This was when Bonnie Prince Charlie (1720–88), known as the Young Pretender, had landed in his homeland of Scotland from his place of exile in France. He had raised an army and was now marching south towards London, determined to recapture the English throne for himself, as the Catholic Stuart heir to the English Crown.

The legend tells that, on his march south, he too came to Liverpool and to Everton village, to take advantage of its strategic location and to plan an assault on Liverpool. Whilst there, the story goes, he stayed in the same cottage that his ancestor, Prince Rupert, had commandeered. It was said that the Scots prince liked to sit in a large, comfortable old oak chair that was believed to be the one that Rupert had used.

However, this is all nonsense! There is no evidence whatsoever that the Young Pretender ever came to Liverpool, let alone Everton. But that did not stop early Evertonians claiming that he did.

Bonnie Prince Charlie. (Liverpool Athenaeum library)

The townspeople of Liverpool had certainly expected him to attack their town, so they erected some defences. They also stationed groups of locally recruited militia, known as the Liverpool Blues, at various points outside the town. In fact, the Liverpool Blues marched off to fight Prince Charlie and he never came to the town.

Next door to Prince Rupert's Cottage, and dating from the eighteenth century, stood Molly Bushell's toffee shop, where she first made and sold the original Everton toffee – but that is another story too!

At this time, the current owners of Rupert's Cottage decided to sell off some of its fixtures, fittings, and furniture. This included the old chair that had purportedly cherished the buttocks of both Prince Rupert of the Rhine and Bonnie Prince Charles Edward Stuart. People flocked to buy these 'historic' artefacts, including Molly Bushell, who outbid everyone else for the famous chair. Now, in addition to bolstering her own backside, Molly employed it as a useful boost to her toffee sales. She charged her customers a few pence to try out the regal chair for themselves. People queued up to sit in the royal chair, especially the tourists who were now coming to Everton village. When Molly died in 1818, her recipe, original toffee pan, goods, chattels, and the Princes' chair were passed down to her family.

In the late nineteenth century, the ancient cottage and the first toffee shop were pulled down to make way for new housing, and Everton became very densely populated. Molly had moved to a larger cottage and shop elsewhere in the village, on Browside.

Soon, all of Everton Hill and Ridge were covered by dense terraces of Victorian and Edwardian houses, tenements, and overcrowded court dwellings. Ancient Everton Village was swallowed up and vanished. Of course, all of these homes went the way of bulldozers in the thorough slum clearances of the 1970s and 1980s. This massive demolition left only open land, which was soon landscaped as Everton Park.

All that remains of the ancient village of Everton are Village Street and Browside (neither with any buildings now standing on them), part of the village green, and the old Everton village lock-up – also mentioned previously.

Interestingly, though, there are descendants of Molly Bushell currently living on Wirral, and they still own Molly's copper toffee-making pan and Prince Rupert's wooden chair, which is still actually known as 'Bonnie Prince Charlie's Chair'!

℣essel ℣umber 290

In 1860, the American President, Abraham Lincoln (1809–65), wanted to abolish the slave trade in his country and emancipate (free) all existing slaves. The states in the south of the USA deeply resented what they regarded as government interference in their affairs. The principal source of wealth for the people of these states came from the crops produced on plantations worked by slaves, such as cotton and tobacco. Britain, and especially Liverpool and Manchester, traded with American slave states in these commodities, even though we had abolished slavery in our own territories more than thirty years previously.

Because of the president's policy, in April 1861 seven states in the Deep South seceded from the Union, followed by four more. They now formed their own federation, which they named the Confederate States of America. They established a new government with overseas ambassadors and adopted their own flag and currency.

The remaining states to the north of the country were named the Union, and their flag was the Stars and Stripes. The American Civil War had now begun and it tore apart the country, communities, and families.

Although the British Government officially supported the Union, behind closed doors they supported the Confederacy. Liverpool did so too, as our economy was so interwoven with trade in cotton and tobacco. This supported jobs for more than 500,000 people, especially across the north of England. Despite this, most British workers supported the Union and the anti-slavery movement.

The Liverpool Chamber of Commerce was actively encouraging the Confederacy. In fact, in October 1864, a fundraising Confederate

Bazaar was held in St George's Hall in the town, with individual stalls named after the various southern states. This ran for five days and raised £20,000 (£1,968,472 today).

Earlier in the war the Confederacy was very short of weapons, so they sent agents to Liverpool, where they were very well received. So much so that in June 1861, an unofficial Confederate Embassy was opened in Abercromby Square and an espionage and naval headquarters in Rumford Place – both buildings survive today. The official American Union Consulate at that time was in Paradise Street, and the American Eagle can still be seen above the entrance today.

The Confederate Ambassador was James Dunwoody Bulloch (1823–1901), and from Rumford Place he arranged the largest single delivery of arms to the Deep South, in October 1861. He also organised and oversaw the construction and purchase of forty-two specially built, heavily fortified, and ultimately very well-armed Confederate warships to attack Union warships and supply vessels. These were built in secret, in shipyards in Liverpool, particularly in that of John Laird & Sons in Birkenhead.

Each new ship was given either a false registration or a code, and the most notorious of these 'secret' ships was named simply

The Birkenhead shipyard of John Laird & Son, where many Confederate warships were built in secret. (Discover Liverpool library)

Vessel Number 290. This was built at Laird's and fitted out in the Great Float at Wallasey.

Vessel 290 was a 1,040-ton, 300hp wooden-screw steamer. She measured 210ft (64m) in length and had a beam of 32ft (9.75m), and she cost the Confederacy £47,500 (£4,474,041 today). She was constructed with reinforced decks for cannon emplacements and with gunpowder magazines below water level.

Under the command of Rear Admiral Captain Raphael Semmes (1809–77), and to help keep the ship a secret and maintain the illusion of Britain's neutrality, *Vessel 290* was not equipped with arms in the shipyard. She quietly slipped out of Liverpool on 29 July 1862, under the false name of *Enrica.* Her crew included 120 volunteers from Liverpool.

Her final arming and fitting out was completed at sea on 24 August 1862, and the American officers now joined the crew and Captain Semmes at sea. A ceremony was held on board, the Confederate flag was raised, and *Enrica* was renamed *Alabama*. She now set sail on active service for the Confederate rebels.

Over the next twenty-two months, Birkenhead-built *Alabama* sank or captured and then burned twenty-five sailing ships, four brigantines, six schooners, and seventeen barques, complete with their cargoes. This was a loss to the Union of property worth over $5.25 million (in sterling this would be £908,326,017 today). In fact, so great was the damage caused by *Alabama* and other Confederate raiders that President Lincoln threatened to hang their crews for piracy should they be captured.

On 19 June 1864, *Alabama* was resupplying and undergoing repairs at Cherbourg in France when the Union warship USS *Kearsarge* appeared off the coast. After what was described as a 'spectacular battle', the Union gunners fired so effectively at *Alabama* that she began to sink and the crew had to abandon her. An English yacht sailing nearby rescued *Alabama*'s Captain Semmes and many of his crew to prevent them being captured by the Americans.

The American Civil War ended in 1865 with the defeat and surrender of the Confederate forces and states. However, the final event of this catastrophic conflict did not actually take place in American waters or on American soil.

On 3 August 1865, Commander James Waddell (1824–86), of the Confederate raider CSS *Shenandoah*, received information that the Civil War had ended. Not wanting to surrender to the Union for fear of imprisonment and execution, he chose to sail 17,000 miles to 'Confederate-friendly' Liverpool.

On 6 November 1865, he anchored his ship in the middle of the Mersey and then lowered his Confederate flag. He next surrendered his ship to Captain Poynter of the Royal Naval vessel HMS *Donegal*, which was also anchored mid-river. Commander Waddell then made his way to Liverpool Town Hall, where he walked boldly through the main entrance. In his hand he held a letter addressed to Liverpool's Lord Mayor John Farnworth Esq, formally surrendering his vessel to the British Government.

This was the last official act of the American Civil War, which ended not in America but inside Liverpool Town Hall.

44

BRITAIN'S LARGEST THEATRE: THE OLYMPIA

In the Liverpool district of Kensington, on West Derby Road and standing next to the Grafton Rooms night club, is the former Olympia Theatre. Built for Moss Empires Ltd, this was modelled on the Kirov Ballet in Moscow by its designer Frank Matcham (1854–1929), the renowned Edwardian theatre designer.

It opened on Easter Monday in April 1905, with a spectacular equestrian revue called 'Tally Ho!' that starred George Formby Senior (1875–1921). It was, at the time, Britain's largest variety theatre and the vast auditorium could seat 3,750 people. These were accommodated in the stalls, dress circle, upper circle, gallery, and in private boxes. The largest theatre in the UK today is the London Palladium, but this can only accommodate 2,286 people.

As an extensively equipped and thoroughly modern concert hall and variety theatre, the Olympia could mount any type of production. And it did so, from comprehensive variety programmes presenting the most famous music-hall stars to spectacular pantomimes, and from boxing bouts to fencing tournaments. Feature films could be shown and classical concerts, ballet, and grand opera were all performed here. Indeed, it was at the Olympia that Liverpudlians first heard Wagner's 'The Ring' and Puccini's 'Girl of the Golden West'. The great dramatic actress Sarah Bernhardt (1844–1923) gave her last performance in the city at the Olympia.

The theatre was also equipped to stage magical extravaganzas using the latest technology. This included a revolutionary hydraulic mechanism that enabled the 42ft-(12.8m) wide arena to collapse in on itself in sections, and to disappear in twenty seconds. Then, and in less than a minute, a lake containing 80,000 gallons of water would replace the arena. This was then the setting for stunning aquatic displays that frequently incorporated flowing rivers and waterfalls. Glittering water pageants saw mermaids riding on the backs of mythical sea beasts. Impressive sea battles could be fought between competing navies, or so it would appear to the amazed audiences.

Circuses were also presented there, and the first dozen rows of seats could be removed to make way for a sawdust circus ring. Animals were transported up to the arena by special elevators from cages in the basement; these included giraffes, elephants, lions, tigers, and even hippos! There were also, of course, horses. One year, and to great public acclaim, the star animal attractions were a pair of high-diving horses from the USA, named King and Queen. These animals ran up a 25ft (7.6m) high, fenced-off walkway, before leaping headfirst into a large tank of water on the stage below! World-famous circus performers appeared in the productions, including Bedouin Arabs showing off their horse-riding skills, Japanese high-wire performers, and Chinese tumbling clowns and acrobats.

The Olympia Theatre, at one time the largest theatre
in Britain. (Discover Liverpool library)

The entire stage was itself a mechanical marvel because it had sophisticated trapdoors and could even move entirely from side to side as well as backwards and forwards. There was also a huge turntable at its centre. The roof could slide open to allow for cooling and ventilation.

Despite, or perhaps because of these costly features, very few productions actually made a profit. In fact, by 1925, the Olympia could no longer survive as a theatre, so it closed on 7 March that year. Its final performances were of *Faust* and *Tannhauser*, given by the British National Opera Company.

This magnificent building was then converted to begin a new life as a 'super cinema'. It reopened as such on 30 March 1925, after only a three-week closure. Its first film presentation was *The Thief of Baghdad*, starring Douglas Fairbanks Senior, and its last presentation was on 29 March 1939, with a showing of *Stablemates*, with Mickey Rooney. This was because, with the Second World War looming, the building was now commandeered by the War Office and used throughout the war as a naval storage depot.

The story of the Olympia then takes many twists and turns. It remained closed and empty from 1945 until 1948, when it was bought by Mecca Ltd. This company refurbished and reopened it as the Locarno Ballroom in 1949. In 1964, it began yet another life as a luxury bingo hall, and it was this that saved the old theatre from demolition. Large sums of money were spent to restore the building to its former glory and, for fifteen years, it survived. During this period, The Beatles appeared here a number of times.

In the mid-1970s, the manager of what had then become the Locarno Bingo Casino was a personal friend. Soon after he took over the running of the vast theatre, he invited me to have a guided tour of every nook and cranny of the building. I eagerly accepted his offer. I was thoroughly impressed with everything about the place, but especially when he showed me a treasure trove of old documents that he had discovered, including correspondence with international performers as well as old playbills and posters.

But then he took me into the basement. There, below the arena, he showed me the vast water cisterns, hydraulics, turntables, generators, effects mechanisms, specialised lifts, and trapdoors and hatches. However, I was particularly fascinated by the surviving original compounds, cages, and feed stores for the animals that once performed here.

Following the redevelopment of the local area, the population rapidly declined and once again the theatre became uneconomic to operate, even as a bingo hall. In 1982 the Locarno was closed and put up for sale and, while it was on the market, it was occasionally used as a film location. In fact, the overtly sexual video for the hit record *Relax*, by the Liverpool group Frankie Goes to Hollywood, was filmed at the Locarno in 1983.

No buyers could be found for the old theatre, which is Grade-II listed, and so, in 1987, the owners reopened it again, but only until 1993. In that year it was bought by Silver Leisure Ltd, who also owned the Grafton Rooms next door. This wonderful theatre then became a sleeping giant, and it lay unused for seven years. This was until, on Easter Monday in April 2000, and with its original name restored, the Olympia reopened as a cabaret, show bar, and nightclub.

Changing hands again, the city's only surviving Edwardian theatre has now reinvented itself as the Eventim Olympia and, following a further major refurbishment, it stages sporting events and a wide range of concert and cabaret performances. Its current audience capacity is 1,960 people

As the community around the Olympia begins to regenerate and redevelop, and as Liverpool itself continues its formidable renaissance, we may yet see the magnificent theatre reclaim its own rightful place as a jewel in the crown of the city's classic entertainment venues.

45

₮HE ₡OST ₷TREET ₿ENEATH ₡IME ₷TREET

For many years, an urban myth has persisted in Liverpool that, somewhere under Lime Street, a street of shops and houses lies buried beneath the modern roadway and buildings. Many tales have also been told of strange noises, eerie sightings, and ghostly goings-on, in and around the vicinity of the Empire Theatre, the old North Western Hotel, and the entrance to the main Lime Street Railway Station.

I had never paid much attention to these tales until, a few years ago, I was contacted by some professional ghost hunters who told me that the underground street did, in fact, exist. They had found the access point and had permission to go down to explore and investigate. 'Did I want to come with them?' they asked. Naturally, I instantly accepted their offer.

I was surprised when the agreed meeting place was the Head of Steam pub, inside the ground floor of the old North Western Hotel. We were a small group of four or five people, and the manager of the bar led us behind the main bar and down to the cellar. There, we found a large, locked wooden door, which the manager unlocked with a proportionally large key. It led to a wide set of stone steps leading down beneath the beer cellar, and the manager then left us to it as we continued down the steps.

They opened onto a wide, long, high-ceilinged corridor that disappeared into the distance. This was dimly lit by some bare light bulbs that hung, every 15 yards or so, from a cable strung from the ceiling. Fortunately, we had brought powerful torches. The passage seemed to run beneath the entire length of the very long hotel, which stands directly across from St George's Hall.

The former North Western Railway Hotel on Lime Street, beneath which was the 'Lost Street'. (Discover Liverpool library)

The hotel is a massive, ten-storey (not including the subterranean areas), twenty-one-bay-long, 330-room, five-star luxury former British Transport grand hotel. It was built in 1871 by the London & North Western Railway company specifically to serve the railway station. Indeed, from the rear of the hotel, residents and guests could walk directly to the main station concourse, platforms, and railway tracks.

The North Western Hotel had been designed to service and accommodate wealthier passengers using the new railway, as well as those bound for ocean crossings aboard the great transatlantic liners leaving Liverpool from the Pier Head floating landing stages. The architect was the renowned Aigburth-born Alfred Waterhouse (1830–1905). He built so many of the city's most significant buildings. These included the University Victoria Building and Clocktower on Brownlow Hill, and the Prudential Assurance Building on Dale Street. He also designed Manchester Town Hall and the National History Museum in London. His passion for using blood-red terracotta stone and brick in his buildings encouraged his architectural colleagues to give him the nickname 'Slaughterhouse Waterhouse'!

Over the main entrance are two tall, costumed, sculpted sandstone figures. The one on the left represents the peoples of Europe and the one on the right the peoples of the Americas. These are just two of the many symbols around the city of the historical, direct, economic and cultural links between Liverpool and the USA.

The people who were now coming to Liverpool on business, or simply to use it as a waystation, included the great, the good, the famous, the rich, the influential, the important (and the self-important), who all required the very best accommodation that the town (soon, in 1880, to become a city) could provide. The latest modern plumbing, bathing with hot water, and flushing lavatorial facilities were a major attraction in the hotel, as were the highest and most tasteful standards in décor and furnishings. Excellent food was served in the elegant surroundings of the silver-service restaurants, enhanced by a most excellent wine cellar. The hotel was in stiff competition with other high-class hotels in the town, but especially with its main rival, the Adelphi, at the other end of Lime Street.

However, tastes and the economy changed and, by 1933, the splendid North Western Railway Hotel had closed. It functioned as small offices for a short while, but soon became empty and closed up, perhaps surprisingly, for over sixty years. Then, on 26 September 1969, it was announced that the building was to be demolished to make way for a new office block! Complaints about this proposal flooded in to the City Council and, in May 1973, the then Liberal MP, now Lord David Alton (b.1951), spoke in Parliament in its defence and the demolition proposal was withdrawn.

However, the building remained closed and unused. Until, in 1994, it was bought by Liverpool John Moores University. They spent £6.5 million to completely restore and refurbish the building as halls of residence for their students in the city. Renamed as North Western Hall, it reopened on 2 September 1996.

At the same time, part of the ground floor of the old hotel reverted to the servicing of rail passengers and this is when what was once part of the main reception and foyer of the hotel became the Head of Steam.

Back in the 'lost street', it soon became clear to us ghost hunters and investigators that what we were walking along had certainly never been a surface street. What it had been, in the days when the hotel was a thriving enterprise, was the service hub of the building. Because of its breadth, the corridor at one time was plainly a major thoroughfare. This meant that it was designed as an important area where a great many people worked and moved about. There were dozens of large rooms and storage areas running off it, as well as doors and short passages leading to more rooms.

There were, indeed, rows of doorways off the 'roadway' that did, to some extent, look like a row of front doors of houses. Some of these had very large window-like spaces in the walls facing the corridor. These could quite easily have been mistaken for shopfronts.

All the walls were of plain brick and stone, with no adornments or embellishments. The rooms were largely empty, except that some had old cupboards, furniture, and the dumped detritus of many empty and purposeless years. It was clear to see, though, that formerly this entire subterranean world had been from where the hotel was managed and run; where the maintenance workshops had been based; the staff fed and watered; the kitchens, cold stores, and larders located; food prepared; crockery and cutlery kept; linens and bedding stowed; the sheets laundered and ironed; the supplies kept; coal stored; and the boilers stoked.

Because we were far below street level there was no natural light, of course, except for what appeared from a small number of shafts in the walls, which allowed some light to filter down from outside the building above. This was an eerie place, still filled with the echoes of the frantic domestic life and activity that at one time fuelled this once magnificent, luxurious palace of privilege.

But, once again, things changed for the old hotel. In 2016, the university sold the building to a development company, who planned to refurbish it as a hotel once more. Their plan fell through, and the project was then taken over by another company. They have now successfully and completely redeveloped and refurbished the hotel once more, at a cost of over £30 million. This has seen the building revert to its origins, but today as the state-of-the-art, twenty-first-century Radisson RED Liverpool Grand Hotel.

The building's grand central staircase, with its 300ft (94m) long handrail has been renewed and refurbished, thanks to the workers who spent 792 hours on its restoration. Glass experts were brought in to reproduce the original 20ft-high (6m) stained-glass window above the grand main staircase. It now has 201 bedrooms, five meeting rooms, and a modern steak restaurant specialising in quality cuts, high-end wines, and hand-crafted cocktails.

The 'lost street' has now indeed disappeared forever, as the subterranean world has also been totally refurbished as a fully functioning basement for service and resources. I am pleased about this and glad that I had the opportunity to discover the truth about the legend for myself. By the way – we did not find anything ethereal on our exploration!

46

BLACKIE, THE WAR HORSE

The sacrifice of so many men and women from Merseyside during both world wars cannot be underestimated nor forgotten. But neither can that of the thousands of animals who were injured or killed on the battlefields. They never asked, nor did they volunteer to take part; we just made them do so.

We may have cared for them or even loved them in return, but many have been forgotten or not considered at all. Carrier pigeons, dogs, mules, donkeys, and camels all played a significant part. Canaries were used to detect poison gas and cats were used to kill rats in the trenches. Monkeys, goats, bears, and even lions were kept as pets or mascots to help maintain morale. Undoubtedly though, thousands of horses gave loyal and devoted service during Britain's wars (again, not that they had much alternative).

At least there are a number of memorials to individual animals across Europe and Britain, including in Liverpool. This includes one near Higher Road in Halewood, on the southern edge of Liverpool, which is dedicated to 'Blackie, the War Horse'.

Born around 1905, Blackie served with the 275th Brigade Royal Field Artillery 'A' Battery, 55th West Lancashire Division, during the First World War. This was with his master, Lieutenant Leonard Comer Wall (b.1896), who was from West Kirby on Wirral. Wall received a military commission and was posted to the Western Front in September 1915.

Whilst riding Blackie, Lieutenant Wall was killed in action on 9 June 1917, at Ypres in Belgium. He was only 20 years old. Leonard was buried at Lijssenthoek Military Cemetery at Poperinge, in the Belgian province of West Flanders. Blackie received severe shrapnel injuries in the same incident, was treated and then sent back to the front, where he remained until the end of the war, in 1918. He bore his visible battle scars for the rest of his life.

After the war, Blackie was bought by Lieutenant Wall's mother, who then loaned him to the Territorial Riding School in Liverpool. In 1930, the horse was retired and stabled at the Horses' Rest in Halewood. He lived here very happily and was loved by local adults and children until his death, aged 37, in December 1942.

Incidentally, for some years Blackie was the lead horse in the Liverpool's annual May Day Horse Parade, along with another ex-war-horse known as Billy. Blackie always wore his late master's medals in the parades.

Blackie now lies in the north-west corner of the western field fronting Higher Road and was buried with his master's medals. This site though, is now being built over with new houses, so it is to be hoped that the horse's grave will be preserved and maintained.

Blackie, the war horse, with Lieutenant
Leonard Comer Wall. (Discover Liverpool library)

47

PRINCES ROAD SYNAGOGUE

The Princes Road Synagogue is an outstanding place of worship and is regarded as being the finest such building in Europe. It was consecrated on 3 September 1874, and at that time was the largest synagogue in Britain with room for up to 900 people.

The late eighteenth century had begun to see a greater tolerance towards religious diversity in Liverpool and, by 1877, there were over 250 sites of worship throughout the town. These represented a wide variety of faiths and doctrines, as well as Protestant and Catholic, and included places of worship particularly dedicated to serving the beliefs of, among many others, the German, Greek, Italian, Polish, and Swedish communities.

Other great buildings were also constructed, providing places of worship for those people in the town other than Christians. Not the least of these was the impressive Princes Road Synagogue. It is a richly decorated and impressive building in an eclectic Moorish Revival architectural style. Inside, it is constructed as a basilica with a high, central nave and side aisles. It has a barrel vault lit by clerestory windows.

The architects, from the Liverpool firm of William and George Audsley, used iron to construct the pillars, which was reportedly unheard of at the time. At the end of the nave, overlooking the wide central space, is a large and beautiful Romanesque rose window. This not only adds light but also emphasises the magnificence of the interior of the building. Below this is the tabernacle, which houses the Torah and other holy books. This too is carefully and reverently decorated and embossed with gold leaf in intricate designs. The Grade-I-listed building is renowned for its painted and gilded interior, complex and multicoloured mosaics, and the liberal use of gold-leaf decoration, fine woods and marbles.

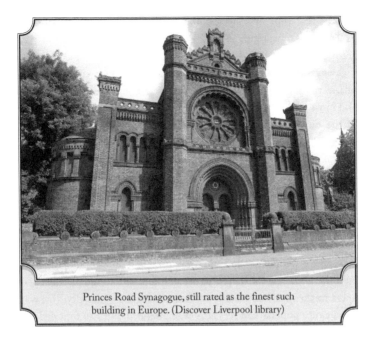

Princes Road Synagogue, still rated as the finest such
building in Europe. (Discover Liverpool library)

Costing £14,975 (£1,311,765 today) to build, the synagogue was
funded by members of the congregation. Indeed, ladies of the Jewish
community in Liverpool held a bazaar and luncheon to raise money
towards the costs. The event raised approximately £3,000 (£262,791
today), which was donated to the synagogue for the decoration of
the interior.

The design of the magnificent building was so well renowned that,
some years later, the Jewish community in London decided that they
wanted a synagogue of the same style. After buying the drawings and
designs, an almost identical synagogue was built in Bayswater, London,
which is still in use today.

The first Jews in Liverpool came to the town in the mid-eighteenth
century and were a small group of itinerant migrant peddlers, probably
of German extraction. Liverpool's was the first Jewish community in
the north of England and, for over a century, it was the largest outside
London. In 1789, the Jewish population of the town stood at 100 people,

and the year 1807 saw Liverpool's first synagogue established on Seel Street, in the town centre. By 1825, the Jewish community had grown to around 1,000 people and, by 1914, to its largest figure of 11,000.

Jews for many generations have been, and continue to be, a vital part of Liverpool life. Many of the city's most famous sons and daughters, and most significant benefactors, have been and are of this faith. One of the most prominent was David Lewis. He was the founder of Lewis's Department Stores, with its iconic sculpture of a giant full-frontal nude man over the entrance to the Liverpool store. Lewis was also a successful marketing expert and extremely wealthy as a result. However, he used much of his wealth for the benefit of the people of Liverpool, as well as being one of the major donors to the synagogue.

Among the many community and charitable organisations he supported financially he created the David Lewis Hotel. This provided inexpensive accommodation and meals for sailors and working men. He built the David Lewis Theatre to bring drama, serious music, ballet and opera to the local community of Toxteth and the wider city. This was always very popular and regularly well attended. He also founded the David Lewis Youth Club, again serving the poorer districts of Liverpool.

Other, recent Jewish benefactors of the city include the late renowned solicitor, Rex Makin; Ian Broudie, the lead singer of the pop group the Lightning Seeds; the late Judge Rose Heilbron QC; former MP Edwina Currie; much missed entertainer and benefactor of youth clubs in the city, of all and no denominations, Frankie Vaughan; and The Beatles manager, Brian Epstein.

However, by the 1950s, the Jewish population of Liverpool had declined to 8,000 and today it stands at approximately 2,000. Despite its respected status, the Princes Road Synagogue also now has a dwindling congregation. Today, it is only attended on Sabbath mornings and holidays, although it remains popular for weddings and bar mitzvahs.

However, the synagogue is a welcoming place for people of all denominations. By arrangement, visitors can tour the building and learn more about Judaism generally, and the history of Jews in Liverpool in particular. The writer H.A. Meek said in his 1995 book, *The Synagogue*, 'He who has not seen the interior of Princes Road Synagogue in Liverpool has not beheld the glory of Israel.'

48

₿IDSTON MILL

A windmill for grinding wheat has stood on Bidston Hill since 1596, and the original 'peg' or 'post' mill was about 20 yards to the north of the present windmill. The first mill was made entirely of timber, including the grinding machinery inside the mill, except the millstones of course! It was manually pushed round on a central post or pillar so that its vanes always faced into the prevailing wind. This was accomplished by the miller and his assistants pushing on a long tail pole that stuck out from the back. Holes were cut into the sandstone rock in a circle around the mill, so their feet could gain some purchase as they heaved the great structure around. These holes can still be seen today!

Then, in 1791, the mill burnt down. During a gale, the vanes were turned so fast by the wind that the friction created in the wooden machinery caused the whole mill to burst into flames. As a result, a new mill was built, but on the present site.

In this new windmill it was the top, or 'cap', that could be turned so that the vanes would face the wind, rather than the entire mill. Inside, a large wooden chain wheel was used to slowly turn the roof around, using a rack-and-gear system, which can still be seen. However, in 1821 this mill caught fire too ... and then again, in 1839!

Milling was actually a dangerous occupation for the people who manned it. In those days, there were two doors on opposite sides of the base of the mill. These led into the ground floor machinery area and the storage space for grain. As the vanes could face in any direction and came close to the ground as they turned, there were times when one door could not be used.

On one occasion, the miller must have forgotten the position of the vanes and used the wrong door. He was struck by the heavy wooden arms as they swept passed the doorway as he was coming outside and he was killed outright.

Another time, an itinerant tinker called to the mill to sell pots and pans. His wares were tied to his donkey, which he left tethered to one of the vanes as he went inside to see the miller. There was no wind so the vanes were static. Whilst the men were chatting the wind unexpectedly got up, began turning the vanes of the mill, and hoisted the unfortunate donkey up into the air. It was then carried around and around!

The frantic braying of the animal and the rattling of the ironmongery brought the tinker and the miller rushing outside to see what was going on. They managed to put the brake on the turning shaft in the mill and so halt the vanes and fix them in position. They were also able to lower the nauseated and thoroughly surprised donkey to the ground. Here, they untethered him, relatively unharmed after his ordeal.

The current mill on the hill ground its last bushel of grain in 1870, and was allowed to fall into decay. It was restored in 1894, but was again badly damaged in 1927, this time by vandalism. This prompted local people to set up a public subscription fund, which successfully raised enough money to recondition the mill inside and out. For many years it was then opened to the public on the first Sunday of every month. That was until 2001, when Health & Safety inspectors closed it down as a dangerous building.

It reopened, though – in 2009 – following a £120,000 restoration and complete refurbishment to comply with legislation. The old mill now forms the hub of the public open space and nature reserve that covers Bidston Hill and its acres of dramatic heathland and woods.

49

THE WORKING MAN'S PAUPER PIONEER

Robert Noonan, who wrote the famous novel, *The Ragged Trousered Philanthropists* under the pen name of 'Robert Tressell', lies buried in Walton Cemetery, in Liverpool. The book, which has been an international bestseller for over a century, tells the story of a working man named Frank Owen. This very ordinary man, along with his fellow workers, is shamelessly exploited by their bosses and upper classes. These powerful men seek to keep themselves in their comfort and their riches, and the poor in their poverty and in their place at the bottom of the class structure of Edwardian Britain.

In the story, Owen fights against this inequality by urging 'collective action', principally through the formation of trade unions and by going on strike. Tragically, however, Robert Noonan was not to live to see his book published or become internationally successful and almost a manual for trade unionism.

Robert Noonan was born on 18 April 1870, in Dublin, possibly as one of four illegitimate children born to a wealthy Protestant landowner. This was Sir Samuel Croker, a retired inspector in the Royal Irish Constabulary and a magistrate, who already had a wife and family. Robert's mother, Mary Ann Noonan, was a young, single servant girl to Croker's family, so was in no position to resist her powerful employer's sexual demands. All four of her children were seemingly fathered by Croker.

Baby Robert was christened as a Roman Catholic, but with his father's surname, and Sir Samuel did pay for his child's schooling. However, this was only for the first five years of Robert's life, because Croker died in 1875. Records are unclear, but he seems to

Robert (Tressell) Noonan, author of
The Ragged Trousered Philanthropists.
(Discover Liverpool library)

have left Mary the income from some properties in Dublin, so she was not entirely destitute. Also, Robert continued to receive a good and full education. He learned not only to read and write but also to speak several languages.

Even so, his family life was hard, and by the time he turned 16 in 1886, he was becoming only too aware of the exploitation of the working classes generally and of the Irish in particular. After Croker's death, Mary Noonan had married a cabinetmaker in London, where she was now living with Robert and his three sisters. The boy did not get on with his stepfather and adopted his mother's maiden name as his own surname. He then decided to run away from home.

There are many versions of the story of Robert's youth and early adult life, and many of these conflict dramatically. Consequently, I have decided to draw mainly on the TUC's History Online website, as this version is likely to be the most authentic.

By 1890, one of Mary Noonan's daughters was working as a live-in servant for Charles Fay Junior, a shipping agent living at Courtney Road, Great Crosby, to the north of Liverpool. Robert was also in Liverpool by then, working as a signwriter and living in Queen's Road, Everton. However, his work was not regular and, in fact, he was nearing starvation. He unsuccessfully turned to crime.

On 27 May 1890, he broke into the home of his sister's employer and stole a quantity of silver and electroplated items. The police found and arrested him, and on 10 June 1890, he appeared at Liverpool County Intermediate Sessions Court at Sessions House, Islington, Liverpool. Robert pleaded guilty to housebreaking and larceny and received a six-month prison sentence. The case caused a minor sensation and was covered by the *Liverpool Mercury* newspaper.

Upon his release from prison later that year, Robert made his way to South Africa in search of a new life. Setting up home in Cape Town, he established himself as a successful, financially secure painter and decorator.

In 1891, he met and married 18-year-old Elizabeth Hartel. They had their only child, a daughter they named Kathleen, who was born on 17 September 1892. It seems that Robert doted on his little girl but his marriage was very unhappy because his wife had a string of affairs. They divorced in 1897, and Robert was awarded all the joint property of the marriage as well as custody of his daughter.

Father and daughter moved to Johannesburg. Here, Robert got a job working for a construction company, again as a painter and decorator. It was at this time that Robert's politics began to become more radical.

Robert Noonan now began to take an active interest in Reforming Socialism and, in 1898, he became a member of a South African group of Nationalist Irishmen, who were fighting British rule in Ireland. He also helped to form the Irish Brigades, who fought alongside the white South Africans against their British colonial masters in the Boer War of 1899–1902.

Again, records are unclear and it is difficult to establish with any certainty whether Robert fought with the brigades, was interned by the British, or left South Africa before the war broke out. Whatever the case, it was around this time that he caught tuberculosis, which was then incurable and usually fatal. It is certain that Robert's health became worse, so, in 1901, he decided to move back to Britain with his daughter, because of the milder climate. He and Kathleen settled in Hastings with another of his sisters, a widow.

Once back in England he could only secure very low-paid work as a signwriter. Again, he witnessed such poverty and exploitation of his fellow employees, and of the English working classes in general, that in 1906 he joined the Social Democratic Federation. This was the first Socialist-Marxist political group to be formed in Britain. But it was at a time when Socialism and trade unions were still fledgling movements, without any form of employment or legal protection, and Robert was fired from his job because of his activism.

Now he had to take whatever bits of work he could find, and life for Kathleen and Robert became very difficult indeed. He found it hard to find money to pay his rent and feed them both but, nevertheless, he was determined to keep himself and his daughter out of the workhouse.

It was around this time that Robert began to write *The Ragged Trousered Philanthropists*. Into his novel he poured his lifetime's experience of the abuse of the working classes by the upper classes and capitalists of Britain. He wrote under the pseudonym 'Robert Tressell' because he was worried that the political views in his novel would only get him blacklisted. He chose the surname 'Tressell' as a reference to his work as a painter and decorator. He took this from the trestle table that had been such a vital tool of his trade.

Completing his book in 1910, he set about trying to find a publisher. But, because the views expressed in it were so radical, this was more difficult than he had imagined. In fact, he was rejected by three different publishers and treated with much scorn and abuse. This left him so depressed that his mental and physical health deteriorated and he made up his mind to burn his manuscript. However, his daughter Kathleen doted on her father as much as he did on her, so she secretly rescued it. She kept it hidden in a tin box under her bed.

All the while Robert's health continued to worsen, so he decided that he and his daughter should go to Canada, to seek a fresh start and a new life, and see if the climate of that country would be better for his health. He only had enough money to take them both to Liverpool, but Robert hoped to be able to earn enough money in the city to buy tickets to sail across the Atlantic.

Father and daughter arrived in the great port early in 1911, and moved into a small room at No. 35 Erskine Street, in the Islington district of the city. However, before he could begin his search for work, he collapsed and was taken to Liverpool Royal Infirmary. There, on 3 February, and to the great distress of his loyal and loving daughter, Robert died.

He was buried, along with twelve other people, in an unmarked pauper's grave pit, in Walton Cemetery in north Liverpool. This is now opposite Walton Prison in Hornby Road. The location of the writer's grave was not discovered until 1970, when an impressive monument was erected on the plot in tribute to Robert 'Tressell' Noonan. This was unveiled by his granddaughter in 1977, and now visitors come here from all over the world. They do so to honour one of modern history's most influential campaigners for workers' rights and one of the fathers of twentieth-century socialism.

Three years after her loving father's death, Kathleen finally managed to sell his manuscript and *The Ragged Trousered Philanthropists* was finally published in 1914.

50

⊕TTER§P⊕⊕L, THE ⊕R⊕M, AND THE L⊕§T C⊕MMUNITY ⊕F JERIICH⊕

The open land at Aigburth Vale, at the left-hand corner of Aigburth Road and Jericho Lane, is named Otterspool. It was once the site of a settlement of ancient Britons alongside a narrow river that still runs here. The Romans came here too, on their way between their strongholds of *Bremetennacum Veteranorum* (Ribchester), in Lancashire, and *Deva* (Chester), in Cheshire. Roman coins and other artefacts have been found in the district nearby.

Records do not say what the river was originally known as, but it was later named the '*Osklebrok*' by the ninth and tenth-century Viking invaders who also settled here. However, after King John came to Liverpool in 1207, this area became part of his vast hunting forest of Toxteth Park, when Otterspool appears in documents as 'Stirpul' and 'Oterpol'. In medieval times, the 'pool' in Otterspool was just that, an inlet from the Mersey fed by the Oskelbrok. Indeed, this was a much smaller version of the great pool that gave Liverpool its name, further north up the coast.

There was a fishery at Otterspool that attracted huge flocks of wild ducks and, of course, the otters. Monks from the monastery at Stanlawe, on Wirral, would have fished here. Codling, whiting, fluke, sole, plus an abundance of shrimps were also caught in the river. Up to the middle of the nineteenth century, numerous fishermen lived on the banks of the Mersey between Dingle and Hale, where fish yards and ice houses were built. Indeed, salmon in the Mersey were so plentiful that, by the late seventeenth century, local fishermen were not only supplying all the towns within 20 miles of Liverpool, but salmon were also being fed to pigs! The nineteenth-century construction of Liverpool's South Docks, the Manchester Ship Canal, and general industrial development around the banks of the Mersey eventually ruined its fine fisheries.

In the early seventeenth century, Puritan exiles from Lancashire towns had come to Otterspool to settle on land that was then owned by the Roman Catholic Molyneux family (later the Earls of Sefton). They generously gave permission for these Dissenting Protestants to establish a community here. They did so around a farm that they established and named Jericho, after the Biblical city. The Puritans also renamed the Osklebrok the River Jordan. The track from Aigburth, past their farm and down to the Mersey, they named Jericho Lane. Indeed, during that time the whole area became known as 'the Holy Land'.

One of King John's two hunting lodges in Toxteth Park, Lower Lodge, once stood against the Osklebrok, near the modern sandstone railway bridge that now spans the footpath through modern Otterspool Park. The long-lost lodge was once the home of the remarkable seventeenth-century Puritan astronomer, Jeremiah Horrocks (1618–41). There will be more about this remarkable young man later in this book.

The River Jordan was actually the continuation of the confluence of two streams. These also still exist and are the Lower Brook, rising from two ponds on land that became the former Botanic Gardens on Edge Lane, and the Upper Brook, which rises in a spring beneath the mid-fifteenth-century Monks' Well in Wavertree Village. Culverted from the village it then breaks ground and feeds into the lake in Greenbank Park. Next feeding the lake in the university halls of residence, the brook runs underground again to then form Sefton Park Lake together with the Lower Brook.

Now forming a single river, it flows out of the lake as the Jordan and under Aigburth Road. Here, it breaks ground for 50 yards or so, behind the low wall and railings at the top of Jericho Lane. It is then culverted once more under the old carriage drive through Otterspool Park. This was actually the original and now dry Oskelbrok riverbed. Following the line of Jericho Lane, the river then joins the Mersey.

Originally, the Jordan fed into the basin of the old Otter's Pool inlet in a 'magnificent cascade'. This basin, which is now filled in, forms part of the modern park, near the café and activities centre.

All of the modern park was once the Otterspool estate of John Moss (1782–1858). He was a banker who founded Moss's Bank at the corner of Dale Street and Castle Street. After his death, this eventually became the Midland Bank and then HSBC Bank. Moss was a slave owner, who inherited 1,000 slaves and a plantation in the Bahamas. The slave trade had been abolished in Britain in 1807, but this did not stop Moss because it was not abolished in British colonies until 1834.

When it was finally and completely banned, Moss received government compensation of £40,353 18*s* 3*d* for the loss of his surviving 805 slaves (equivalent to £2,237,216 today). He also, in 1838, imported 414 indentured labourers (another form of slavery) from India to work on his plantations. Eighteen died on the voyage and a further 100 were dead within five years.

Moss's Otterspool estate was quite large and he had acquired it after it had passed through the hands of a number of local aristocrats, as well

Otterspool House, the home of John Moss. (Discover Liverpool library)

as the Molyneuxs. By 1812 he had built a grand mansion house for himself, overlooking the Jordan, named Otterspool House. From here, he also supervised a snuff tobacco mill he had also built on the banks of the pool, and ground the crops grown on his own slave tobacco plantations, making a great deal of money.

John Moss was also the first chairman of the Liverpool & Manchester Railway Company. As we have seen, this was the world's first passenger railway, which was designed and built by George and Robert Stephenson. George was a great friend of Moss and stayed with him at Otterspool during the construction of the railway line. The Stephensons also tested out their rail tracks and the *Rocket* using scale models on a scale track. They laid this out as the world's first model railway along the dry riverbed of the Jordan, which was then Moss's carriage drive and is now the main pathway through Otterspool Park.

From 1915 to 1930, well after Moss had died and his estate had been sold, a very popular menagerie opened at Otterspool. The paying public came to see lots of fascinating animals and birds, but the biggest attractions were a one-eyed badger and a toothless lion. Moss's old mansion served as the zoo's offices.

In 1930, the entire estate was bought by Liverpool Corporation. The Otter's Pool was filled in and the land levelled and redeveloped as the large, rolling, well-laid-out and landscaped park that we have today. Otterspool house was pulled down the following year

The park, its carriage-drive pathway, and Jericho Lane all lead to a wide, 5-mile-long pedestrian-only riverside walkway. This borders the park and is named Otterspool Promenade. It was created entirely on land reclaimed from the Mersey, and was the idea of Liverpool's outstanding city engineer, John Alexander Brodie (1858–1934). John also invented prefabricated houses, dual carriageways with central reservations for tramways, and nets for football goals, among much else. The Queensway Mersey Tunnel from Liverpool to Birkenhead was also his idea. This opened in the year of Brodie's death.

The promenade began with the building of a high sea wall in 1929. The wide space between this and the existing shoreline was infilled with 2 million tons of household waste and ashes from tens of thousands of Liverpool homes. This had to be one of the world's first genuine recycling projects. The scheme took twenty years to complete but 'The Prom' and park were opened to the public in 1950, with the phrase, 'Wealth from waste, and beauty from ashes'.

As one walks along the Promenade, along the sea wall and looking out across the river to the Wirral Peninsula, one is not only doing so on top of rubbish, but also over the bedrock of the River Mersey! The product of the excavations of Queensway – the rock, rubble, and clay – was also dumped here as part of the reclamation of the land. In fact, spoil and rubble from the Wallasey 'Kingsway' Tunnel lies under the road that now runs from the end of the Prom, at the bottom of Jericho Lane, into Liverpool city centre. This is the appropriately named Riverside Drive, which was itself a major reclamation project, this time in the early 1980s.

Liverpool is no longer the place of 'dark satanic mills' of late-twentieth-century misconception, but a city and suburbs of 'green and pleasant land', and with a remarkable history, as Otterspool proves.

51

NAKED ABANDON IN AND ON THE MERSEY

The Georges and Princes floating landing stages on Liverpool's riverfront were built in 1847, at what we now know as the Pier Head. Before this, though, to get on and off the ferry boats, passengers had to walk to the end, or 'head', of a long, narrow, fixed wooden pier, hence 'Pier Head'. This did not rise and fall with the tides and so was dangerous at the best of times, especially for women with large frocks!

The original repaired ferry pier, adjacent to Mr Wright's bathing pools, built to re-home the naked swimmers. (Discover Liverpool library)

But it was even more treacherous when they were distracted by the regular sight of naked boys and young men swimming and diving, splishing and sploshing, splashing and flashing, all around the pier. The wearing of bathing costumes was very much a mid-nineteenth-century invention and, during the eighteenth and early nineteenth centuries, nude male disportment near open water and rivers was quite commonplace. Girls and women did not indulge in this sort of exposed pastime unless they were of the 'lower orders' of society!

However, this nakedness still shocked many people, especially women of the middle and upper classes, who were known for their more sensitive, or perhaps easily thrilled, dispositions. As a result, female ferryboat passengers often fell into the Mersey in shock (or amazement). So, in 1765, a seawater swimming baths was built to try to dissuade the nudie bathers from publicly displaying themselves around the area of the pier.

This was built by a local boat builder by the name of Wright, who saw an opportunity and decided to diversify his business interests. For a small fee, and in complete naked privacy inside a basic, purpose-built building, men and women (at separate times) could choose from two swimming baths into which river water was piped. One of these was a cold pool whilst the other was heated, which was quite an innovation for the time.

If, however, patrons preferred to swim in the river itself, they could also do so in a section of the riverfront that Wright had enclosed with a palisade of high, rough wooden planks, standing about 30ft (9m) square. This area was accessed by a short deck from the main pool building, and when the tide was high this created a safe plunge pool.

Despite these amenities, a great many would-be swimmers either could not afford or did not want to pay to swim in 'their' river. So the nudie bathers simply moved further north to disturb the people of Bootle! This was before the building of the North Docks, when all that stretch of riverfront was still beach.

Mr Wright's baths were taken over in 1794 and run by Liverpool Corporation, but were demolished in 1817 to make way for the construction of Princes Dock. The street behind the new dock became known as Bath Street, the name it still has today.

Another way of avoiding giving offence to more susceptible Liverpudlians was to remove swimmers to a safe, completely isolated swimming place in the middle of the river. On 11 June 1816, a privately financed, large, flat-bottomed ship was launched named *The Floating Bath*. This had been built with an open upper deck shaded by a large awning in high sunshine for promenading and sunbathing. There were also two coffee rooms selling 'all sorts of refreshments at moderate prices'.

On the enclosed lower deck there were changing rooms and private cabins for secluded relaxation. These surrounded a large, tank-like swimming bath that measured 26ft (8m) by 82ft (25m). It was 7ft (2.1m) deep at one end and 3ft (91cm) at the other and was constantly fed by the tidal flow of the river as it passed through the ship from stem to stern.

Opened originally only for male patrons, a regular rowing boat ferry service transported swimmers between the Pier Head and the bath. The entrance fee was sixpence each, which included the boat to and from the bath and the use of towels. However, following pressure from the women of the town, for limited hours on two days each week only, *The Floating Bath* was opened for the exclusive use of female bathers! Now males and females could happily swim at separate times, modestly attired in bathing costumes if they wished, or in complete, uninhibited, natural abandon if preferred, and without fear of frightening the horses!

A year after the launching, on 25 April 1817, the following announcement was made in the *Liverpool Mercury* newspaper:

> Liverpool Floating Bath: T. Coglan respectfully informs his friends and the public that the FLOATING BATH, which has undergone some useful alterations, and is newly painted etc. will be brought into the River the first favourable opportunity, and, for a short period will be moored opposite the Parade, near the situation lately occupied by the Princess frigate, after which it will be moved to a more advantageous position at the entrance to George's Dock-basin, which Dock, it is expected will be closed about the middle of May. Boats belonging to the Bath will regularly attend at the Parade-basin.
>
> Tickets for the Season to be had at all the Booksellers on the terms of last year.

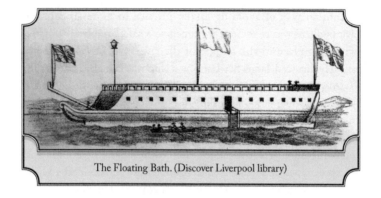

The Floating Bath. (Discover Liverpool library)

The same guide also described the activities of some of the patrons of this water-borne swimming pool:

> Very often swimming matches are got up impromptu, to come off in the open river, and many an exciting scene has been witnessed as, perhaps, when six lusty swimmers plunged in simultaneously, manfully contesting for some little prize subscribed for on the occasion. There were two Hebrew gentlemen who frequented the baths at one time who were admirable swimmers, performing all sorts of antics, jumping into the open river from the upper part of the bath deck, and turning somersaults before entering the water. These young men would remain under water so long as to alarm their friends and spectators, which would only be allayed by seeing them rise to the surface at some far different point than was anticipated. These exhibitions of natation were, however, discontinued when the number of ferry steamers increased.

The Floating Bath remained a popular attraction and conversation piece for over a decade, but it became redundant when, in 1828, Liverpool Corporation invested a considerable amount in the construction of a new state-of-the-art swimming complex. This was built on George's Parade, overlooking the place where the floating ferry landing stage would later be constructed and where the Mersey Ferry Terminal building stands today.

52

THE CAFÉ ON TOP OF A CHIMNEY

What was originally named the St John's Beacon Tower is now known as the Radio City Tower. It stands above St John's Retail Market, in the heart of Liverpool city centre, at a height of 450ft (137m).

It was built in 1965 as a luxury restaurant on top of a chimney. When the market was opened in the same year, the smoke from the incinerators that burned the waste from the two floors of small traders' stalls was carried away through this colossal pipe, high above the city. However, within a few months of the beacon/chimney coming into action so did the 'Clean Air Act'! This made such rubbish burning illegal, and so the chimney part of the beacon immediately became redundant.

Fortunately for the building's owners, the high-class tower summit restaurant that was an integral part of the design remained completely legal and fully functional. As did the observation deck and café on the roof of the restaurant, which completely encircled the top of the tower. A high-speed lift carried people directly up to the restaurant level, and then continued up to the roofless open observation deck behind windswept 6ft (1.8m) high railings, and enjoy a light snack or a pot of tea in the small café – weather permitting, of course. Or, if they had plenty of money, they could dine in the posh restaurant on the deck below.

With luxurious fixtures, fittings, and design, all in contemporary 1960s styling that, for no apparent reason, had more than a smattering of tartan, this was a state-of-the-art, modern restaurant. It was planned to not only stun the tastebuds with outstanding food, but stagger the senses as well.

The tables and seating were spread out around the entire perimeter behind great sheets of plate glass. These afforded a 360-degree vista of the city of Liverpool and almost the full length of the Mersey. On a clear day, the estuary and Liverpool Bay could be seen, together with the Wirral Peninsula and Wales beyond, plus all the land for miles around. The views are still spectacular from the top of the tower today.

However, the greatest innovation in the Tower Restaurant was that the dining area was mounted on a great turntable. This completed a full circuit once every half an hour, which was quite a novelty – although diners could have some difficulty in locating their table and fellow diners on a return trip from the lavatory!

The food was extremely expensive and, despite the company's ambitions, was actually of poor quality, with a limited menu and unimaginative presentation. I know this from first-hand experience. Liverpudlians of taste and discernment stayed away in droves, and the restaurant began to lose money. Then, in the early 1970s, the restaurant stopped revolving after the main turntable bearings seized up. Also, the upper observation deck had to be closed down for safety reasons.

Next, in 1977, a fire damaged the lift, which meant lengthy repairs. The tower and restaurant had to remain closed whilst work went on. Another fire, in 1984, this time in the restaurant itself, finally convinced the owners to shut the tower down completely.

In the late 1990s, however, it was bought by the commercial radio station, Radio City. The entire tower was completely renovated. The observation deck was roofed over, weatherproofed, and redeveloped, along with the restaurant level, as the company's headquarters, administration centre, and broadcasting studios. These opened in 2000.

The giant turntable still does not work, even though all the machinery remains in place beneath the floor of the studio level, where the restaurant once was. Nevertheless, the studios do move – because the Beacon sways about 18 to 24in from side to side in the wind. This means that studio staff members really do keep supplies of anti-sickness tablets in their desks. I also know this at first hand, being a regular broadcaster from these highly elevated studios.

Perhaps this was another reason why the restaurant wasn't popular – were the diners getting seasick?

The Radio City Tower, previously St John's Beacon – the restaurant
and café on top of a chimney. (Discover Liverpool library)

53

SECRETS OF THE BEATLES' STATUES

Across Liverpool, but mainly in the city centre, can be found a number of statues of The Beatles – John Lennon, Paul McCartney, George Harrison, and Ringo Starr. Some are more representative than others, but the very first was unveiled in 1974.

Created by Liverpool's own radical, anarchic, eccentric, left-wing and wonderfully talented sculptor, Arthur Dooley (1929–94) and titled 'Four Lads Who Shook the World', this complex piece hangs on a wall in Mathew Street, at the heart of the city's Cavern Quarter and opposite the Cavern Club. In this very impressionistic composition, the figure of the Madonna represents Liverpool as the mother city. She holds three babies to symbolise John, George, and Ringo. At first, there was a fourth baby with wings, representing Paul and originally situated to the left of the Madonna. This was stolen in 1975. It did turn up again, however, thirty years later, but has not reappeared on the sculpture. After John Lennon's murder in 1980, a baby holding a guitar was added, inscribed with the words 'Lennon Lives'.

There are a number of statues of John Lennon around Liverpool, including an excellent one on Mathew Street outside the Cavern Pub. Sculpted by local artist David Webster and unveiled in January 1997, John leans on the Cavern Wall of Fame, which lists all the performers who ever appeared at the world-famous club. This statue is particularly popular with tourist photographers.

Another image of John stands at Liverpool's John Lennon Airport. At 7ft (2.1m) tall, the magnificent bronze was sculpted by one of Liverpool's most prolific and respected sculptors, Tom Murphy, and unveiled in March 2002 with John's widow, Yoko Ono, and the then prime minister's wife, Cherie Booth QC. The recently redeveloped airport was then formally opened, renamed, and dedicated to the Beatle in July 2002 by the late Her Majesty Queen Elizabeth II.

The first sculpture of the complete group was erected in 1984 above the door of The Beatles Shop, at No. 31 Matthew Street. It consists of busts of the four 'Mersey Mop Tops' looking down on the passing crowds. Although in need of some restoration, these fairly accurate portraits of the boys were funded by Beatles fans worldwide and were sculpted by David Hughes.

In the same year, Paul McCartney's brother, Mike (b.1944), unveiled the John Doubleday statue, on 26 April. This stands in the main atrium of the former shopping and office complex in the Cavern Quarter, named Cavern Walks. At the unveiling, Paul's brother allegedly asked, 'Which one's our kid?' – and, let's be honest, these are not the most realistic images of The Beatles on display in the city!

On North John Street stands the four-star Hard Day's Night Hotel. It claims to be the only Beatles-themed hotel in the world and, on the outside of this building, 30ft (9.2m) above the pavements, stand the 7ft (2.1m) tall statues of the Fab Four. Also sculpted by David Webster, these were unveiled in 2007, and are more like caricatures of The Beatles than portraits. Because of their more cartoon-like design, they are quite controversial among Beatles fans and opinion about them is still divided in Liverpool.

Other sculptures can be found in 'The Beatles Story Exhibition' at Albert Dock, where they are sculpted in wax and were originally on display in Madame Tussauds in London. But giving the Cavern Walks statues a run for their money, in terms of limited accuracy, is the group sculpture on display inside the Rubber Soul Bar on Matthew Street.

However, by far the very best images of the greatest ever rock group can be found at Liverpool's Pier Head waterfront. Unveiled on 4 December 2015, these statues are slightly larger than real life. They are beautifully and accurately sculpted by Andrew Edwards. The 1.2-ton sculptures are cast in resin and clay and were gifted to the city by the owners of the Cavern Club. However, they each bear a secret symbol that is particularly associated with each group member.

First, look very closely at John's hand. Resting in his palm and almost hidden by his fingers two acorns can be seen. In June 1968,

Yoko Ono and John Lennon planted two acorns in the garden of Coventry cathedral. The couple said that these represented their wish for world peace. After they married in 1969, the couple sent pairs of acorns to leaders across the world, asking that the 'living sculptures' be planted as a symbol of world peace. John, of course, was murdered by a gunman outside his New York home in 1980, at the age of only 40.

Next, take a close look at Paul. In his hand he carries a video camera. This is an acknowledgement of his marriage to Linda Eastman, the American photographer, musician, animal rights activist, and entrepreneur. She was also a renowned vegetarian, which philosophy she and Paul adopted in 1971. Linda became a highly respected photographer, notably of performers and celebrities, and also joined Paul as a musician and singer in his group, Wings. Married in 1969, they had four children and were idyllically happy. Tragically, Linda McCartney was diagnosed with breast cancer in 1995. She died in 1998, surrounded by her family.

Now, take a look at the back of the group, and get really low down to take a look at the sole of Ringo's shoe. Cut into the shoe is the figure '8'. This refers to Ringo's birthplace at No. 9 Madryn Street, in the Liverpool 8 postcode district of the Dingle area of Liverpool.

Finally, and still viewing the figures from behind, take a look at George's overcoat belt. On this are inscribed in Sanskrit the words of the Hindu Gayatri Mantra, which translate as:

Om the divine light
Please guide our mind to the divine
So we can experience it within and around us
To live the divine life

George became a devout, practising Hindu after the time that The Beatles spent with the Indian guru, Maharishi Mahesh Yogi in 1967. His faith always meant a great deal to him until his untimely death from lung cancer in 2001.

Not only have The Beatles, as individuals and as a band, left an incredible musical and cultural legacy across the world, but they remain a vital part of Liverpool's history and heritage in so many ways. They really were – and still are – The Fab Four. The statues at the Pier Head celebrate all of this.

The Beatles' statues at Liverpool's Pier Head.
(Discover Liverpool library)

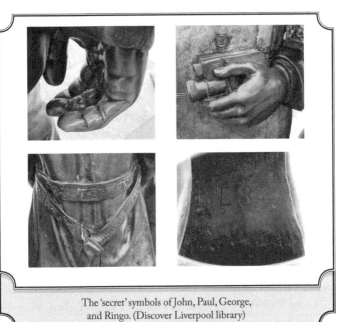

The 'secret' symbols of John, Paul, George,
and Ringo. (Discover Liverpool library)

54

THE ANCIENT CHAPEL OF TOXTETH

Puritan farmers escaping from persecution in and around Bolton, as we have seen, established and settled at Jericho Farm at Otterspool. They also set up more farmsteads in the Dingle area of Toxteth.

The Puritans were religious Dissenters, people who felt that the Protestant Reformation of King Henry VIII (1491–1547), which began in 1534, had not gone far enough. They wanted to purge the new Church of England of what they regarded as the 'Popish idolatry' in the ceremonies and rituals that it had inherited from the Catholic Church. The name was originally applied to them as a form of contempt but, in due course, and because of its association with 'purity', they adopted the name themselves.

In 1611, they built a schoolhouse at the bottom of Park Road in Dingle. They needed a schoolmaster and they invited Richard Mather (1596–1699) to accept the post, even though he was then only 15 years old. Richard was successful and popular, but then he went away to complete his studies at Brasenose College at Oxford.

In the meantime, the Puritans added a chapel to their existing schoolhouse that, from the 1830s, has been known as the Ancient Chapel of Toxteth. Richard returned home, this time as their minister, and he preached his first sermon in the newly built chapel in 1618, at the tender age of 22.

However, persecution had followed the community from Bolton and was also becoming intolerable in and around Liverpool. Eventually, they had to escape. Richard Mather and many Toxteth Puritans travelled from Liverpool to Plymouth. From there, in 1635, they set sail to the New World of America with the Pilgrim Fathers. Mather's ship was tiny and named *Mary and John*.

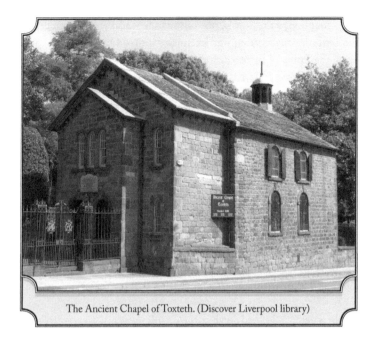

The Ancient Chapel of Toxteth. (Discover Liverpool library)

Once in America, he continued to preach in Massachusetts, until his death in 1669. Richard's son, Increase Mather (1639–1723), and his grandson, Cotton Mather (1663–1728), became presidents of Harvard and Yale Universities respectively.

Bizarrely, Increase and Cotton indulged in persecution themselves, when they prosecuted, found guilty, and executed poor girls and women, and some men, in the notorious Salem Witch Trials of 1692–93. In all, twenty people and two dogs were hanged. One person was pressed to death under rocks for refusing to testify.

In the days when Park Road was just a track leading to what had been King John's Toxteth Hunting Park, the Dingle Brook ran through the district, passing through a rocky dell giving the Dingle its name. Local tradition has it that during the English Civil War (1642–51), Cromwell's troops camped in and around the chapel to get shelter, and to water themselves and their horses from the Dingle Brook. They were Puritans themselves, so would have been welcomed by the local people.

As mentioned previously, one of the other significant members of the Toxteth congregation was Jeremiah Horrox. Often referred to as being the 'father of British astronomy', he had been born at Otterspool in Toxteth Park, in 1619. A follower of Ptolemy, in 1639 Jeremiah built an orrery, a moving model of planetary motion. He was the first person to predict the transit of Venus across the face of the sun, and to accurately calculate the distance from the earth to the sun.

Jeremiah died in 1641, aged only 23, and was buried at the chapel. A memorial tablet inside the building was erected in 1891 and pays tribute to him. On display in the World Museum Liverpool is a mock-up of his telescope, together with his original notebooks.

There are many other funeral and memorial tablets and stones in and around the chapel. Perhaps one of the most poignant is dedicated to the daughter of Dr Matthew Dobson, from Harrington Street in the town. He was a founder member of the Liverpool Academy of Painting and Sculpture in 1769. The inscription reads:

> She is dead, my beloved daughter Elisa.
> My pretty, winsome, kind-hearted daughter is dead,
> Very simple she was and withal very intelligent,
> Accomplished and well-read, pure in heart – spiritually minded,
> And she is dead.
> Farewell, dear Elisa, farewell.
> Always will you be regretted by your grieving father,
> Regretted but, thanks be to God, not lost to me,
> For a happier day will dawn when I shall see you again, my daughter
> And live with you for ever and ever.
>
> Matthew Dobson to his dear sweet and blessed daughter Elisa
> Who, at the age of seventeen, And in the year of Our Lord 1778,
> Departed peacefully to heaven.

In the burial ground behind the chapel is the Colybarium, a porticoed passage with niches for bones and funerary urns. This was where the wealthiest members of the congregation were buried. It includes some members of the Holt shipping and Rathbone merchant families.

Also, members of the Melly family are buried here. They are ancestors of the late George Melly (1926–2007), the well-known local artist and jazz singer. George's great-uncle, Charles Melly (1829–88), was a great benefactor to the needy of Liverpool, always giving parties for the poor and especially for children. He established sickness funds and savings clubs for his workers, and in the 1860s, with William Rathbone, he raised funds for impoverished Lancashire cotton workers.

In 1852, local police officers told Charles that poor Irish immigrants were asking them where they could get water, as they had to drink from horse troughs. At his own expense, Melly installed taps at Princes Dock and then twelve drinking fountains at Liverpool's railway stations, with a further forty being installed throughout the town. In 1857, Melly provided strong oak benches throughout the city to 'allow the poor to rest from their burdens'.

In 1868, he provided public playgrounds and four public gymnasiums, even paying for the equipment and the wages of the instructors. In the same year, he established Sefton Park Lake and persuaded the Corporation to open the park on Sundays, which before this time was unheard of. Most of the members of the chapel congregation were similarly engaged in philanthropic works on Merseyside and elsewhere, and this continues today.

The last burials in the chapel graveyard were made around 1960.

The Ancient Chapel of Toxteth is a Grade-I-listed building and its design was deliberately plain, simple, and completely unadorned. There are no icons or religious imagery whatsoever, and certainly no altar cross or ornaments. Inside, there is a pulpit against the east wall, also north and south galleries, and sets of box pews dating from 1650 and 1700. All the seating is of plain wood and is deliberately uncomfortable.

This is the oldest Dissenting place of worship in Britain and, although substantially rebuilt in 1774, parts of the original walls remain. It was in this year that most members of the congregation adopted the doctrine of Unitarianism, which has been the denomination of the chapel ever since. In 1840, the old schoolhouse was demolished, to be replaced by the present vestibule, porch, vestry, staircase, and organ loft. The Ancient Chapel of Toxteth is another of Merseyside's important, culturally significant, and fascinating historical gems.

55

₮HE ₴TEBLE ₣OUNTAIN ᵁRCHIN: ₳ ₴AZZ ₱IONEER

Adjacent to St George's Hall and the Wellington Column, at the top of William Brown Street in Liverpool city centre, is the Steble Fountain. This Grade-II*-listed monument was donated to the City by Lieutenant Colonel Richard Fell Steble (1825–1876), who had been Lord Mayor of Liverpool in 1874/75. Sadly, he died before this imposing water feature was unveiled in 1879.

The fountain is an iron and bronze casting of an original statue that was designed by sculptor Paul Lienard for the Paris Exposition of 1867, but this original now stands in Boston, USA.

In the picture, taken at the fountain in 1895, note in particular the little, barefoot boy, fourth from the left. His name is William Gordon Masters, and he had been born in shabby court housing in Eldon Place off nearby Scotland Road, on 5 June 1887.

Growing up in a family of mixed heritage, life was especially tough for young William. His Jamaican father, a sailor, died in a steamship accident at sea whilst the boy was only nine years old, and William himself had nearly died of pneumonia at the age of four.

Even as a very small child William earned money by selling newspapers, but mostly by entertaining and singing on the streets or in pub bar rooms. Passionate about music and music halls, when he was five William sneaked into a show at the Haymarket Music Hall in Liverpool. Whilst enthusiastically singing along to the show one of the performers recognised him and invited William onto the stage to sing, which he readily did. To the delight of the audience he sang 'The Honeysuckle and The Bee'. Over the next few years he sang often at the Haymarket. Then, at the age of nine, an important impresario named

William (Gordon Stretton) Masters (fourth from the left) from the slums of Liverpool, who taught and wrote for the stars and pioneered jazz music across South America. (Discover Liverpool library)

William Jackson heard about this, and invited the young entertainer to join a touring clog dancing troupe of boys he managed, known as the 'Eight Lancashire Lads'. One of the other members of this troupe was a young Charlie Chaplin, well before he got his break in films.

In 1903, William Masters changed his name to Gordon Stretton, using his middle name and a variation of the surname of a popular American singer, Eugene Stretton. It was also in this year that his mother died of cancer.

By this time, Gordon (William) had become very proficient as an instrumentalist on a range of instruments, and went touring with the clog dancers for a short while.

At the age of seventeen he returned to Liverpool where he appeared in pantomime, in 1904-05. This was starring the American star Billie Burke (1884-1970), the wife of impresario Florenz Ziegfeld (1867-1932). She became best known for playing 'Glinda the Good Witch', in the 1939 film, 'The Wizard of Oz.'

By 1908, at the age of twenty-one, Gordon was touring Britain as a leading member of the 'Jamaica Native Choir.' They appeared in many venues including, ironically, in St George's Hall! Little did William realise what the future was now going to hold for him, as a young man who had been born in the slum courts of Liverpool.

He then began performing as a jazz drummer, from around 1910, and for a time he played with William Dorsey's Band from the USA. They had come to Britain to present two jazz shows – 'Dusky Revels' and 'Darktown Jingles'– and Gordon led the band when Dorsey fell ill. But then World War One broke out, in 1914.

By 1915, Gordon had joined the Army, but he was badly wounded at Amiens and hospitalised. Here he met an Irish Nurse named Molly Smith. She cared for Gordon and they fell in love. He was honourably discharged and the couple returned to England to convalesce.

As soon as he was fit Gordon returned to his music and was successful enough to have his own company of dancers. In 1916, he appeared with them in the highly successful hit run of the musical comedy/pantomime, 'Chu Chin Chow', at her Majesty's Theatre, in London's West End.

Gordon's success and fame grew and he returned to touring music halls and jazz clubs in London. However, despite his popularity and achievements, Gordon was still a black man in a white society. He decided that he and Molly would move to Paris, where there was a real love of jazz and being black was much more accepted and less of an issue. In fact, he had now become so well-known and his music so loved that here people would stand in respect as he walked into restaurants. In 1921, Gordon and Molly married in Nice. They never had children.

In Paris he met the legendary, black, singer and dancer, Josephine Baker (1906–1975), who was starring in 'La Revue Negre'. Gordon not only performed in her shows but helped with her choreography. He recorded jazz music for Pathé whilst in France, and appeared in shows across the country throughout the 1920s. From time to time he also travelled to New York to perform and, in 1921, here he recorded as a member of the 'Syncopated Jazz Band', also known as 'The Syncopated Six', who released a recording of his songs. Throughout this time he learnt to speak French and Spanish fluently.

In the late-1920s, Gordon and Molly decided to settle in Buenos Aires, Argentina. By now he was an outstanding and world-renowned musician leading his own jazz orchestra. Here he became the 'toast of the town,' and was touring all over South America whilst still performing occasionally in New York and Paris. He later went on to write songs for Vera Lynn (1917-2020); broadcast regularly on the radio; play for and befriend the future King of England, Edward VIII (1894-1972); teach the Brazilian Samba singer and film star, Carmen Miranda (1909–1955), how to sing and dance; and become known as 'the man who brought jazz to Latin America'.

Gordon died in 1982, aged 95, and a long way from being barefoot at the Steble Fountain in Liverpool. In fact, his reputation and popularity was such in South America that, shortly before his death, he was singing in a show in Buenos Aires.

So, whilst Gordon's pioneering life story might not have directly affected Liverpool and its people, his story does show that anyone, regardless of background or heritage, and who has the drive, ambition, and talent to make a real difference can do so, especially if you come from Liverpool or Merseyside!

ACKNOWLEDGEMENTS

I certainly hope that you have enjoyed this new collection of *Even More Merseyside Tales!* There are still so many more where these came from …

Of course, it would not be possible to produce such a broad collection of stories without help and support. I therefore pass on my sincere thanks to the staff of Liverpool Central Libraries and the Liverpool Record Office, in particular, as well as the librarians and many of my fellow proprietors of the Liverpool Athenaeum.

I would also like to acknowledge the unstinting generosity of my fellow members of many local history and Facebook groups across Merseyside.

For their support and stories, I wish to particularly thank the Earl of Derby DL, the late Sir Alan Waterworth KCVO, the Most Reverend Justin Welby, Archbishop of Canterbury and former Dean of Liverpool Anglican Cathedral, and Ken Rogers, journalist and author. I am, as always, very grateful for their encouragement, time, and friendship.

SELECT BIBLIOGRAPHY

Anon., *A Guide to Liverpool, 1902* (Liverpool Libraries and Information Service, 2004).

Bailey, F.A., and R. Millington, *The Story of Liverpool* (Liverpool Corporation, 1957).

Belchem, John (ed.), *Liverpool 800* (Liverpool University Press, 2006).

Buildings of Liverpool (Liverpool Heritage Bureau, 1978).

Cavanagh, Terry, *Public Sculpture of Liverpool* (Liverpool University Press, 1997).

Chandler, George, *Liverpool* (BT Batsford Ltd, 1957).

Charters, David, *Great Liverpudlians* (Palatine Books, 2010).

Chitty, Mike, *Discovering Historic Wavertree* (Wavertree Society, 1999).

Cooper, John, *Liverpool Firsts: Great Merseyside Geniuses* (Sigma Leisure, 1997).

Hand, Charles, *Olde Liverpoole and its Charter* (1907) (facsimile edition: Book Clearance Centre, 2005).

Hatton, Peter, *The History of Hale, Lancashire* (P.B. Hatton, 1968).

Hinchliffe, John and Ian Wray, et al., *Liverpool: World Heritage City* (The Bluecoat Press, 2014)

Hird, Frank, *Old Lancashire Tales* (Memories, 2000).

Hird, Frank, *Old Merseyside Tales* (Memories, 2000).

Hollinghurst, Hugh, *John Foster and Sons: Kings of Georgian Liverpool* (Liverpool History Society, 2009).

Hughes, Quentin, *Liverpool: City of Architecture* (The Bluecoat Press, 1999).

Jackson, William, *Herdman's Liverpool* (The Gallery Press, 1989).

Jones, Ron, *The Beatles' Liverpool: The Complete Guide* (Ron Jones Associates, 2006).

Kelly, Michael, *The Life and Times of Kitty Wilkinson* (Liver Press, 2000).

Lewis, David, *The Churches of Liverpool* (The Bluecoat Press, 2001).

Lewis, David, *The Illustrated History of Liverpool's Suburbs* (DB Publishing, 2014).

Liverpool History Society Journals (various).

Power, Michael (ed.), *Liverpool Town Books 1649–1671* (Record Society of Lancashire and Cheshire, 1999).

Randall, David, *The Search for Old Wirral* (Countyvise Ltd, 1993).

Richardson, Andrew F., *Well I Never Noticed That!*, Parts 1 and 2 (West Derby Publishing, 1995).

Rimmer, Ralph, *Around Wallasey and New Brighton* (The History Press, 1996).

Robson, Martin, *Not Enough Room to Swing a Cat* (Osprey Publishing, 2018).

Stonehouse, John, *The Streets of Liverpool* (British Library Historical Print Editions, 2011).

Whale, Derek, *Lost Villages of Liverpool*, Parts 1, 2 and 3 (T. Stephenson and Sons, 1984).

Williams, Peter Howell, *Liverpolitania* (Merseyside Civic Society, 1971).

For equivalent values in modern day currency, the Bank of England Inflation Calculator has been used: www.bankofengland.co.uk/monetary-policy/inflation/inflation-calculator

ABOUT THE AUTHOR

Born and bred in Liverpool, Ken Pye retired in 2016 as managing director of his own leadership development organisation, The Knowledge Group. This followed a varied career spanning over fifty years, working in each professional sector. This included time as a residential child care officer for youngsters with profound special needs; a youth and community leader; a community development worker for Toxteth; the north-west regional officer for Barnardos; the national partnership director for the Business Environment Association; and as senior programme director with Common Purpose.

He also undertook a special, one-year contract for Liverpool Hope University as executive director of continuing professional development, before setting up The Knowledge Group in 2009.

A proprietor of the Athenaeum for twenty-two years, Ken is also a Fellow of Liverpool Hope University.

Ken continues as the managing director of his own local history company, Discover Liverpool, which he established in 2005 in parallel with his other roles. As such, he is a recognised expert on the past, present, and future potential of his home city and region. Ken is also a frequent contributor to journals, magazines, and newspapers. He is in great demand as an after-dinner speaker and guest lecturer to a wide range of groups and organisations.

Ken is a regular broadcaster for both radio and television, and performs his very popular one-man theatre shows a couple of times a year.

Well known across Merseyside and the north-west as an expert in his field, Ken is the author of many books.and, as well as *Even More Merseyside Tales*, Ken's other published works are:

A Brighter Hope (about the founding and history of Liverpool
    Hope University)
Beastly Merseyside
Discover Liverpool (three editions)
Liverpool: A Potted History
Liverpool at Work
Liverpool Murders and Misdemeanours
Liverpool Pubs
Liverpool: The Rise, Fall and Renaissance of a World-Class City (the
    complete history of the city, also in its third edition)
Liverpool's Military Heritage
Merseyside Tales
More Merseyside Tales
The A to Z of Little-Known Liverpool
The Bloody History of Liverpool (now in its third edition)
Two Triangles: Liverpool, Slavery, and the Church

Ken was a significant contributor to *Trinity Mirror*'s celebration of
Liverpool and its people, *Scousers*, and the special advisor on *Sung and
Unsung*, a collection of portrait photographs and biographies of the
'great and the good' of Liverpool. He also completed two books that
were privately commissioned by the 19th Earl of Derby.

A set of Local History illustrated factsheets have also been published
by Ken, together with a separate set on Traditions and Tales of
Christmas. Ken also produced a set of eight, DVD documentaries on
Liverpool's history, as well as a set of four, audio CDs, on which he tells
his wonderful, curious and amazing tales of Merseyside.

On a personal basis, and if pressed (better still, if taken out to dinner),
Ken will regale you with tales from his own fascinating life, including
his experiences during the Toxteth Riots; as a child entrepreneur, bingo
caller, puppeteer, the lead singer of a 1960s pop group, an artists' and
photographers' model, and a mortuary attendant.

Ken is married to Jackie and they have three grown-up children:
Ben, Samantha, and Danny.

Visit Ken's website at www.discover-liverpool.com